THE RED COROLLA

MONTESSORI COSMIC EDUCATION

Susan Mayclin Stephenson

THE RED COROLLA, Montessori Cosmic Education
Copyright © 2019 by Susan Mayclin Stephenson

FIRST EDITION

Other books in this Series:
The Joyful Child: Montessori, Global Wisdom for Birth to Three
Child of the World: Montessori, Global Education for Age 3-12+
No Checkmate, Montessori Chess Lessons for Age 3-90+
The Universal Child Guided by Nature
Montessori and Mindfulness

Author's website and blog: www.susanart.net

Michael Olaf Montessori Publishing Company
PO Box 1162
Arcata, CA 95518, USA
www.michaelolaf.net
michaelolafcompany@gmail.com

ISBN 978-1-879264-22-9

Photographs, drawings, and cover art by the author

—

What is a Cosmic Task? During a lecture in Ulaanbaatar, Mongolia I was asked to give a description of Dr. Montessori's idea of a *cosmic task*. I explained that, especially during the elementary (ages 6-12) years, when a child is introduced to the creation of the universe, the evolution of life on earth, and the culture of humans, he becomes aware of how everything is connected in some way, how each element has a task that fulfills his own needs and at the same time can contribute to the good of the whole.

I looked down at the edge of the stage where there was a beautiful bouquet of flowers. One variety had bright red corollas composed of several large, flat petals.

"Look at this flower. The color red, the shape of the flower, and perhaps the odor of the nectar, has evolved to attract just the right kind of pollinator that is needed by this specific flower. The flatness of the petal might give the pollinator a place to land to prepare for his work. While sipping nectar the pollinator will brush up against the stamens of the flower and some of the pollen on the stamens will become stuck to his body. He will then fly to the next red flower for another drink and the pollen will fall onto the head of the pistil where it will be drawn within and begin the process of forming seed.

So while the pollinator is meeting his nutritional need, he is also meeting the need of the flowering plant to create seed and spread the species. And what else? The beauty of the flower has provided happiness and smiles for each one of us here at our Montessori workshop.

We shall walk together on this path of life, for all things are part of the universe and are connected with each other to form one whole unity.

— Montessori

OTHER BOOKS
IN THIS SERIES

CONTENTS

INTRODUCTION

Here is a brief overview of how the different areas of the Montessori casa dei bambini, house of children, or primary class for children from age 2.5 to 6 came about.

Sensorial Materials

When she worked with problem children, Maria Montessori began to research specialized educational approaches. She developed materials to help children isolate, and then name and use, concepts experienced by their senses of sight, touch, hearing, taste, and smell. These "sensorial materials" are found in Montessori primary classes around the world today.

Practical Life

Maria Montessori discovered the value of *practical life* exercises during her experiment with poor children in the San Lorenzo quarter, Rome. In the children's environment, called Casa dei Bambini, the children had been supplied with the sensorial materials and beautiful toys — but once they were able to do real everyday work, learning how to be clean, to take care of each other, to sweep and wash and in other ways care for their environment, they became like "new children". They were able to focus and concentrate for long periods of time. They were proud of themselves and what they were learning. Much of this work we know today improves the work of the brain having to do with planning, completing work, focusing, and other skills that are far more predictive of happiness and success in life than IQ. It is common for parents to see the value of academic work, but not that of activities like cleaning, polishing, teaching peers. Modern brain research is helping all of us understand why the practical life area of the Montessori experience is so important.

Language, Math, and Geometry

When those first *Montessori* children returned home after a day in the Casa dei Bambini, they taught their parents what they were learning. They had a new awareness of the real world of senses and showed curiosity about color and taste and beauty. They were becoming more and more adept at new skills: how to take care of their appearance, to be clean, to keep the home clean, to prepare food, to clean up after projects. The parents came to Maria Montessori with a request: They hadn't realized that their children had the potential to be the kind of children they were becoming, and were impressed with this potential that had, until then, not been noticed. Since these poor children would not have the opportunity to go to good schools, the parents asked Maria Montessori if she could teach them academic subjects along with the other work they were doing. So, being a scientist and wanting to help to discover the potential of the children, Montessori started researching and discovered how to combine what she had already learned about the children—that they needed to be free to move, to make choices, to work without interruption — with the possibility of their learning more academic subjects. Today, reading, writing, math, and geometry are standard subjects at this age. They are not required, and they are not taught by the children watching and listening to an adult, but they are successful, solidly, and happily learned by children in a Montessori class.

Culture Subjects

Culture is a term used in the Montessori world to describe the world as given to the child according to his stage of development. Included are the physical and biological sciences, history and geography, dance, music, and art.

Perhaps she was inspired by the request of the San Lorenzo parents to teach their children to read and write. Perhaps it was memories of how she herself had been educated, certainly in good schools but no doubt in the traditional methods of memorizing those things that were selected by someone else. Whatever the reason, these culture subjects soon became an important part of the Montessori experience, at all ages. This is what Maria Montessori said herself:

"Since it has been seen to be necessary to give so much to the child, let us give him a vision of the whole universe. The universe is an imposing reality, and an answer to all questions." (*To Educate the Human Potential*, p. 5)

This book describes these culture areas that are, in my opinion, essential for a complete Montessori education.

The sensorial work gives the child the tools, the refinement of the senses, to experience his world. The practical life exercises help the child learn how to handle and care for, pay attention to, and learn about, his environment. Writing and reading provide tools to classify the world by naming, to express thoughts, to record, to carry out research, and to communicate to others the world he is learning about through the culture lessons. Math and geometry sharpen the mind in many ways, creating order and awareness of similarities and relationships within the world we give to the child.

In the next chapter you will read an article about the Montessori idea of Cosmic Education. This is a term that is used to describe the curriculum of the Montessori elementary child, from age 6-12, where an understanding of the history of and the existence of the universe is made logical, or *cosmic*, rather than *chaotic*. It pulls together the creation of the universe, solar system, and the earth, with the evolution of life on earth, and the development of all elements of human civilizations, and the interrelationship of all of this.

The foundation for all of this is laid during the early years, from birth to six years.

My Own Story

How did I become so interested in this? Here is my own personal, Cosmic Education story. My mother was a musician. "That is an F sharp Susan," came the voice of my mother from the kitchen as I practiced the piano. She played piano, harp, organ, and directed our church choir. She arranged for musicians to perform in the community center in our small Indiana town. Otherwise I might have grown up thinking that music only came from recordings instead of from the human body.

She loved great literature and reviewed books for the newspaper. When I was in high school, frustrated by assignments to read only chapters of great books and then having to analyze them rather than enjoy them I asked her to recommend a book that I could read at home. Her suggestion was *Les Misérables*, by Victor Hugo; I still have that book.

My father was a scientist and engineer. On weekends, to earn extra money and because he enjoyed the work, he installed electricity in homes that were under construction. My job, from a very young age, was to sit at the bottom of a wall, sometimes wrapped up in warm clothing against the cold of winter in unheated buildings and wait for the little piece of metal attached to the electrical wire to drop through the space between the wooden outside wall and the pads of insulation. Then with my father feeding the wire from the floor or attic above I "pulled" the wire through to the bottom of the wall. My love of physics came from the enjoyment of helping my father and his explanation of construction and electricity.

In summers I helped my grandmother (who with my grandfather lived on a farm outside of town) to gather tomatoes and corn from the kitchen garden and feed the animals. Sometimes we rode in the truck along the long bumpy country road to an orchard where we spread blankets under the walnut trees while my grandfather climbed up into the branches to shake down the nuts.

I was free to climb to the top of any tree on the farm. I sat on a stool and watched the cows being milked, stayed away from the pigs, gathered eggs, and looked through the haylofts in the barn to find the kittens we had heard from below. At night my sister and I would curl up in the upstairs bed listening to our grandmother below play the harp and sing us to sleep.

During university I worked at a bookstore. My job was to check all of the books and to gather the slips that said, "This is the last copy," in order to keep all of the sections of the store stocked. This exposed me to the enormous number of subjects that had been written about. I quickly moved out of my comfort zone and started reading in subjects that I otherwise would not have been exposed to. During my sophomore year of college I traveled for 4-months through Europe, the Middle East, North Africa, and Asia. It became clear to me that all humans on earth have essentially the same basic needs, emotions, and goals, and that the variety of ways these needs are met within cultures is the true wonderment of humanity.

It was during my years of Montessori 0-3, 3-6, and 6-12+ training and teaching that I started to see how all of this information was connected. I realized that a broader understanding was making me a more open, patient, understanding person. And this made me want to know more! Montessori's concept of cosmic education taught me how important it is for a well-educated person to have a broad base of understanding.

When you finish reading this book I hope it will help you follow your own curiosity and share old and new passions and interests with children. I hope that the ideas presented within these pages are not just added to a list of things children should do. These days children are busy enough and often overscheduled.

What I remember as the most important and happiest times of childhood and adult life was, and is, having time to think, to wander in nature, and to curl up for hours with a book. The world needs specialists to be sure, but I believe it is in developing an understanding of how everything is connected, how all of us are connected, that will help solve the world's problems and create a better future for all.

COSMIC EDUCATION

THE CHILD'S DISCOVERY OF A GLOBAL VISION AND A COSMIC TASK

By Susan Mayclin Stephenson, Adapted from: The NAMTA
Journal, Vol. 40, No. 2, Spring 2015

*S*usan Mayclin Stephenson tackles a large subject, Cosmic
Education, which Montessori defined as a "unifying global
and universal view(s) of the past, present and future." Stephenson
takes the reader from birth to the end of the elementary age with
examples of how the child grows into an understanding of Cosmic
Education through experiences at home and at school. Central to her
thesis is the theme of discovering one's cosmic task, which depends
on "fostering . . . curiosity and compassion toward other beings,"
Stephenson concludes with examples from around the world and
illustrates how children are born with the tendency toward
compassion and how it is experienced from birth through age twelve
within Montessori environments.

The word *cosmic* today usually means something very
large or having to do with the universe. But the word comes
from the Greek *kosmikos,* from *kosmos,* meaning order. The
term *Cosmic Education* in Montessori lingo refers to a child's
gradual discovery of order, a unifying global and universal
view of the past, present, and future. It is the coming together
of many components of knowledge into a large vision or
realization, as in a mosaic, of the interdependence of elements
of the solar system, the Earth, planets and animals, and

humankind. The character of our time is sometimes referred as the *information age*; today's children are bombarded with facts and information with no way to make sense or bring this information into some kind of order. Cosmic Education helps a child make sense of all the information and is more important today than ever before.

The term *cosmic task* refers to a way for a human being to find a valuable role in this mosaic of life. It is a role that fulfills one's own physical, mental, and spiritual needs and at the same time contributes in some way to the creation of order or balance in the cosmos. It can create a personal expression, and responsibility within this beautiful mosaic of life. Simply, this means we want to help a child learn about and make sense of his world and find a way to make it a better place.

These principles of Montessori education are usually discussed in reference to the second plane of development, the years 6–12. But such an idea is not something Dr. Montessori invented for the elementary child as an academic curriculum. As usual, she "followed the child" and the child's interests. This does not begin at age six.

LEARNING ABOUT THE WORLD

In all Montessori environments — the home, the nido (first year), infant communities (age 1-2.5), primary through high school — curiosity in its variety of expression is fed.

Birth to Three Years

The child's first world is his home. From the first days of life, a child is exploring the world around him, through sight, sound, smell, taste, and touch. This curiosity is a strong urge throughout life, if it is protected and nurtured. Since the beginning of the Assistants to Infancy program in Rome in 1947, parents have been guided in preparing environments that support and feeds this curiosity. It is suggested that the environment of the child not be changed during the first year of life if possible. The child is exploring the order of this environment, his first world, visually from day one and he has a drive to move toward objects and explore them in order to make sense of them. And there is a strong impetus to learn to crawl, stand, and then to walk in a familiar place.

When a child is first on his tummy and able to reach out for a toy, the adult can encourage exploration and movement by placing a toy at a distance that is not so far as to frustrate the infant, yet not so close as to allow him to grasp it with no effort. This skill at observation and meeting the needs of a child is something new parents can enjoy learning. Today Montessori Assistants to Infancy are teaching this and other skills all over the world. Neuroscientists are discovering the value of careful observation of children, and meeting their needs, in these early days and months of life.

Age 3-6 Years

The child's world at this age moves from the family to the primary class. The world is brought into the class rather than the child taken out into the world at this age. We do not believe in pushing a child toward early intellectual studies, however, if presented correctly, young children show a keen interest in a wide range of subjects, which many adults find hard to believe. I learned this the hard way. One year, in my work as a Montessori assistant to infancy, I was consulting with a mother from South Africa about the care of her newborn. As we talked more and more about the Montessori principles supporting what I was sharing with her, she asked if it would be possible for her to observe in a Montessori class. I set up an observation with the local AMI primary class and agreed to meet with her the next morning to discuss what she saw.

I let her talk about all of the things she was amazed to see. She had been raised as a Waldorf child and not introduced to academic subjects until age seven. She was surprised to see children at such young ages teaching each other and doing math, reading, writing, continent puzzle maps, and so on. I could tell that something was bothering her, however, and asked what it was. Hesitantly she said, "Well, it was a very nice situation in many ways, but when do the children get to do what they want to do?"

She was very surprised to hear that the children, after entering the classroom and greeting the teacher, are free to choose any piece of material that they understand. She could not believe that they had actually selected work in areas that in traditional schools they might not, such as math, language, science, and geography.

Before age six, the child absorbs — totally, easily, without effort, and with deep love — all the attitudes and impressions in the environment. It becomes a part of him and forms his mind, so parents and teachers as models are the strongest element in these years. If kindness and patience, enjoying reading, having good manners, enjoying math and biology, for example, are in the environment at this age, these attitudes and actions will be of great value to the child. If they are not part of the early environment, many of these things can be learned later, but they will not make up the basic personality of the child.

Before age six, the lessons and experiences of Cosmic Education are carried out by means of a lot of movement and sensorial experience. But along with the basic and extremely valuable practical life and sensorial lessons, the child begins to learn about the earth and water, physics, plants and animals, the variety of humans on earth, art, dance, music, geometry, math, and language. By the end of this first plane of development, the child has a lively curiosity about and love of all of these areas of study.

Maria Montessori understood the child's built-in receptiveness to all these areas of interest and found that the young child could comprehend what was considered far beyond a child's reach, given the right environment, the right equipment, and a teacher who was skilled at putting the child in touch with this environment.

Age 6-12 + Years

Learning about the world is different at this second stage of development. The environment at this age widens. Rather than bringing the world into the classroom, there are field trips, and the children go out into the world. The more the primary, elementary, and middle/high school teacher knows about the first three years, the more Montessori (as opposed to "traditional") his or her teaching will be. The more secure the teacher of older children is in the fact that curiosity, exploration, work, and effort are natural human traits, the more likely he is to allow the children freedom from an imposed curriculum in order to develop fully and uniquely as a human being. In the second plane, or the 6–12 stage, the child explores more with his mind and on projects requiring teamwork in planning, execution, and presentation.

Social scientists today are well aware of the fact that the standard curriculum valued in traditional school is indeed outdated. We do not even know what professions are going to be of value in ten years, so how can we pretend to know how to prepare children academically for such an unknown future?

There are many lists of "skills for the future" being compiled today. The following skills are found on many of these lists: exploration, putting forth maximum effort, the ability to focus or concentrate, self-control, the mathematical mind, respect of others, the ability to work together, care for the environment. Most of us are going to see immediately that these are skills fostered in a true Montessori environment.

These things are at the center of the Montessori curriculum at all ages and take priority over an academic curriculum. If not, then the outdated standard curriculum can rear its ugly head and turn a school into a very nice school, but not a Montessori school. The teacher and administrator must be extremely knowledgeable of and trusting of Montessori in order to hold back the onslaught of natural parental fear of what will happen if the day is not full of teacher-centered requirements, schedules, textbooks, and homework!

The foundation for academic elements of the elementary Cosmic Education curriculum begins early. One goal of Montessori primary (age 3-6) education is to help children create a sensorial global vision. Children at that age naturally take for granted that what they see in their environment has always been there. It is only later that they will reach an understanding of how things change over time. At age 6-12 the exploration, rather than being limited to what can be explored right here and now with the senses, reaches back into the past and out into space through the means of the imagination — a skill that is not part of the first 0–6 stage of development.

In the first two weeks of the year in the 6–12 class, all of the new students are given the great lessons that introduce the creation of the solar system and earth, the variety and evolution of plants and animals, the stages of human existence, the development of language and math sciences, and the way in which all of these elements of life are connected. The older children almost always choose to attend these lessons and the six-year-old sees the continued excitement of a twelve-year old, which makes these lessons even more interesting. Appreciation for the universe itself is based on the knowledge that it was not always there. Children gradually develop an understanding and gratitude for the universe and their part within it.

Aside from the very limited state or country requirements for each of the six years, the child is set free to explore and to make his own path through the labyrinth of knowledge on

Earth. That is the most exciting part of teaching in the elementary years as the older the child; the less contact with the adult is necessary in a Montessori elementary class. We are there as guides for the child to make contact with experts and sources of knowledge that help further research and creation.

We do not hold him back with hours each week of requirements, schedules, and other limitations. But we must be able to explain why to the parents. In the end, it is the work of the child, who with freedom will go far beyond what we could possibly require, that will convince the parent and the world of the value of this kind of open-ended, out-of-the box education. And it just might be what will solve the problems of our continually changing world.

Here is an example of the difference in the study of geography. In a traditional school, a teacher might assign each child or a group of children to choose a country of the world and do research on it. Then perhaps the child will write a paper that the teacher will read and assess, or the child may give a presentation to the class. And this was all the adult's choice, not the child's.

In a Montessori class I taught in California, a student came in after a field trip we had taken to research local fauna. This child discovered that a fellow classmate, Sierra Miwok, harvested acorns from the Black Oak tree for food! He wanted to know what other Native Americans ate and then wanted to know more about the differences in the daily life of various groups. I reminded him of the civilization study charts that another child had used to study Ancient Rome. This led to studies by other children of other Native American groups, which led to research on why they settled where they did, which led to a new look at the Bering Straits, and then the ice ages, and then to the reasons for migrations of various civilizations throughout history.

Teaching Montessori at this age is guided not by knowing more than the students, but in firing their imagination and their natural curiosity. It required the ability to watch carefully for the tiny nugget of interest and to offer, but not take over, tools for further discovery.

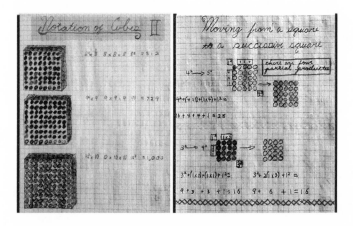

Here is a page from a child's journal, where she recorded a balance of 6-12 work over the years in a beautiful way. These journals are often kept for many years because they are so interesting and lovely.

Recently our Montessori granddaughter was studying journals her mother had made during her own Montessori elementary years. Finally she said, "What does priceless mean?" I replied, "It means that something is so valuable that

no amount of money could convince a person to give it up."
She said, "These books are priceless."

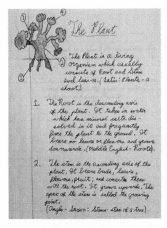

Sometimes teachers may back off from encouraging the child's freedom of exploration and choice of work, because of not knowing how to keep track of this learning or being uncertain of how the child will keep track of his work. But, aside from the short list of local academic requirements for each year in the 6–12 class—that are always available to the children—there is no need to limit or control exploration or to record everything explored. How far do we think Leonardo da Vinci or Einstein would have gotten if they were required to record everything they did? They recorded what they wanted to remember. Children will do the same. They will record meaningful discoveries in journals, with careful drawings, lovely handwriting, and even decorated margins.

For more information on the work of the 6-12 class, see the chapter, "Transition to the Elementary Years," in the book, *Child of the World: Montessori, Global Education for Age 3-12+*.

This natural curiosity and desire to learn more and more, when supported by the best Montessori environment and teaching, is evident in Montessori schools all over the world.

Speaking at the University of Amsterdam in 1950, Dr. Maria Montessori said:

> *It should be realized that genuine interest cannot be*
> *forced. Therefore all methods of education based on centers*
> *of interest which have been chosen by adults are wrong.*
> *Moreover, these centers of interest are superfluous, for the*
> *child is interested in everything.*
>
> *A global vision of cosmic events fascinates children, and*
> *their interest will soon remain fixed on one particular part*
> *as a starting point for more intensive studies. As all parts*
> *are related, they will all be scrutinized sooner or later.*
> *Thus, the way leads from the whole, via the parts, back to*
> *the whole.*
>
> *The children will develop a kind of philosophy which*
> *teaches them the unity of the Universe. This is the very*
> *thing to organize their intelligence and to give them a*
> *better insight into their own place and task in the world,*
> *at the same time presenting a chance for the development*
> *of their creative energy.*
>
> (Polk Lillard 75)

The discovery of *Cosmic Education* and one's *cosmic task* depends on fostering the curiosity of the human being and the natural tendency to feel compassion toward other beings beginning at birth. There is evidence that natural curiosity and feeling responsibility for others, or *compassion* (the sympathetic consciousness of others' distress together with a desire to alleviate it) begins long before the child enters the elementary class. Wanting to be useful and helpful and caring about the happiness of others is not something that needs to be taught; it is a basic part of the human make-up and can be observed even in the very young.

Birth to Three Years

Here is a child safely and securely holding a sibling on the Montessori "topponcino" which is part of the AMI 0-3 training.

During my AMI 0–3 training in Denver, I observed births in Cristo Re Hospital in Rome, Italy. One of the women I observed was well-trained in the Respiratory Autogenic Training birth preparation method that is still part of some assistants to infancy teacher training courses. Even though it was her first child, this young woman was so well trained to relax between contractions that the birth was almost painless and her child was born far more peacefully than is often the case. It was the practice for a newborn to be wrapped up from head to toe and placed in a warm bed in the nursery for a little time after birth. So, I observed the first baby, who had not even cried, snuggle into the warm bed in the nursery and go back to sleep. Suddenly she started to wail loudly the minute another baby in the nursery started to cry!

Since then I have talked to many people who have observed this phenomenon. I have seen very young babies mirror the faces of their adults: I frown, he frowns; I stick out my tongue, he does the same; I smile or laugh, he smiles or laughs. One day I was filming children in an infant community in Denver, Colorado. At one point it was possible to hear a child, far off in the distance outside the classroom, crying. Suddenly the little boy I was filming, who was not much older than two years, got up from his table and chair and announced to whomever would listen, "Somebody needs help!" (Seen in the DVD *Wonderful Two's*.)

Age 3-6 Years

Caring for the school, inside and out, is traditional in many countries, and always part of the Montessori curriculum. This picture is from a school in Thailand. In the primary class, some of the first lessons are how to care for each other and the environment, and children love mastering these skills. If he has not learned this in an infant community, the child learns to cook food and then put it in a special place to share with his friends at a meal. He learns how to walk carefully around the space on the floor or at a table where another is working and to not interrupt his friend's concentration. The children learn how to clean and care for these materials, and to put them back on the shelf in perfect condition for the next child, which is a first act of social caring.

Age 6-12 Years

The teacher of older children, from age 6-12, who has seen this natural caring and compassion in the first six years will be grounded in the knowledge and importance of modeling. The teacher will value opportunities for helping and serving each other above the requirements of an outdated curriculum.

At this age there is a natural interest in fairness and justice in the classroom and in the world. The level at which children can care for each other and for plants and animals and can go out into the world is much higher. They can clean the beaches and riverbeds, feed the homeless, cook their own meals, and clean the school. When there is a temptation to focus on the academic curriculum at this age these things must be kept alive.

> *The child who has felt a strong love for his surroundings and for all living creatures, who has discovered joy and enthusiam in work, gives us reason to hope that humanity can develop in a new direction. Our hope for peace in the future lies not in the formal knowledge the adult can pass on to the child, but in the normal development of the new man.*

> *This is precisely what allows us to believe that a great possibility still lies before us, that there is still one hope for our salvation — a normal development that, fortunately, does not depend on what we attempt to teach the child. What we can do is investigate this phenomenon with the objectivity of the scientist, study the facts that determine it, discover what conditions are necessary to produce it, and keep following the path that leads to normality. What we can and must do is undertake the construction of an environment that will provide the proper conditions for his normal development.*

*The child's psychic energy, once awakened, will develop
according to its own laws and have an effect on us as well.
The mere contact with a human being developing in this
way can renew our own energies. The child developing
harmoniously and the adult improving himself at his side
make a very exciting and attractive picture.*

*This is the treasure we need today — helping the child
become independent of us and make his way by himself
and receiving in return his gifts of hope and light.*

*In this new picture, the adult will appear not only as the
builder of the external world, but, even more importantly,
as the protector of the moral and spiritual forces that
appear anew in every human being born.*
— Montessori, *Education and Peace*

As we can see in the above words by Dr. Montessori, all
of the things we are talking about, such as the desire to learn
and care for others, are not something we teach. They are
above all the *normal condition of the human*. Through the
meeting of their needs according to the stages of development,
respecting curiosity and choice, and the modeling and valuing
of the non-academic skills, children are led naturally to make
sense of the world and to think about their future in terms of a
cosmic task. This is true preparation for life in the Montessori
way.

References

Montessori, Maria. *Education and Peace*. 1949. Oxford: Clio, 1992.

Polk Lillard, Paula. *Montessori Today: A Comprehensive Approach to Education from Birth to Adulthood*. New York: Schocken Books-Doubleday, 1996.

MIND THE GAPS

M*ind the Gap* is a phrase from the London Underground in the UK. It is a warning to be careful of, or "mind", the gap between the train door and the station platform. It brings back memories of spending a year in London with my first teacher-training course.

I am using the phrase in a different way, suggesting that we "mind" or "be careful of" or "fill in" the gaps in our own knowledge as we prepare ourselves to give the world to children according to their stage of development.

We all have special interests, talents, passions, that we love to share with children. But children come to us with their own special talents, their own potential. If we only share music and botany in our classrooms, what about the child who was born to be a physicist? Or if we avoid music because somewhere long ago someone told us we couldn't sing, we are not meeting the needs of the child who longs to compose.

One of the most exciting elements of being a Montessori teacher over the years is the responsibility for continued growth. The more we explore all areas of knowledge, the more we fall in love with them, and the more we are able to construct the puzzle about how everything is related. Children will follow our lead and love them too.

Art is one of the areas in which teachers sometimes think they need to have a special talent in order to create and inspire children. In Morocco in 2018 I gave a lecture on art during an AMI Primary Course. I combined a PowerPoint presentation of art with the experience of exploring making art in just four areas: drawing, painting, paper cutting, and collage.

The only assignment was that the teacher trainees use all of the materials, and that they create an artistic representation of both a flag and a bird. I chose the latter to show anyone can draw a bird in some fashion (so please keep the adult-generated bird outlines for children to color in out of the classroom!!) and because children at this absorbent-mind-time easily learn the names of continents, countries, capitals, and flags of the world. And when a teacher has drawn or painted, and learned about, flags of the world, the children will be excited to do the same.

This was just to get them started since many declared that they are not artists. However, by the time for the midmorning break they asked if they could continue with art after the break. With permission of the director of training they continued. As the announcement of lunch was announced not one person looked up. So we received permission to continue after lunch. As the students completed their assigned work, I told them they could combine any of the methods, paper cutting with collage, drawing with painting, continually reminding them, as I remind myself when I am at home in my studio painting, "It is your piece of paper and you can do whatever you want with it." At the end of the day the students were refreshed, not tired. They would have stayed on.

This experience served two purposes. The first one was expected: they reclaimed confidence in artistic abilities. But perhaps even more important, this day of art was a wonderful introduction to what it feels like to be a child in a Montessori class. There were no interruptions to concentration and the learning did not pass from teacher to student, but from the student's own interaction with the environment.

There were no rules about how their bird should look or how their flag should be made—drawing, painting, paper cutting, collage—and the student experiments with all of the possibilities. They experienced the pleasure of mind and hand working together in a purposeful activity, and again, deep, uninterrupted concentration—all day long. How would they have felt if I had said, as they were deeply settling into the inspired experience of flow, "Okay, put your work away and come and sit with me in a group and listen to me talk so I can teach you something."?

Eagle

But if we do not, as adults, have a balanced view of, knowledge of, and passion or love of all of the areas of the universe — physical and biological sciences, the arts, history and geography — our sharing of these elements of the world risks being dry and uninteresting, and the children at this age will absorb our attitude toward what we are trying to share even more than the lessons we give.

I think it was with the purpose of lighting a flame of passion in us adults, in my first Montessori training course in London so long ago, that we spent many weeks at the beginning of the academic year exploring and rounding out our own knowledge.

There are three areas to help fill in the blanks that I am going to share with you. They are:

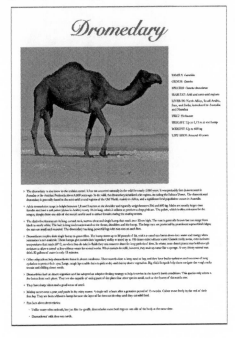

1. General Knowledge

An album that we created during the training and added to over the years. It awakened an interest in many areas of knowledge.

2. The Leaf Album

Again, something we created during the training and added to when we returned to our own countries from England

3. The Poetry Anthology and Cards

We were in the country where English began, the perfect place to learn about the poems, songs, nursery rhymes, and so on of the English Language. So we began our anthology and cards and, more than the other two albums above, added to it continually during out teaching careers.

西江月·夜行黄沙道中

辛弃疾

明月别枝惊鹊，清风半夜鸣蝉。稻花香里说丰年，听取蛙声一片。

七八个星天外，两三点雨山前。旧时茅店社林边，路转溪桥忽见。

【年代】：唐

【作者】：张志和

【内容】：写农村夏夜的优美景色

For the general knowledge album we were sent all over London investigating the natural and manmade world, researching famous people, trees and flowers, and the artists and great works of art in the museums of London. For the Poetry Anthology we reached back into our own childhood to rediscover the favorite poems and nursery rhymes, to share our memories with each other, and then to discover the history of children's literature in London, the capital of the English language. For the leaf collection we learned to look at this part of the natural world through the eyes of children. We did not focus on the local names but on the shapes of the leaves, the attachments of leaves to stems, the patterns of the veins, all of the things that are easily observed by a child under the age of six.

None of us ever looked at the world again in the same way as before this discovery began. Personally, as I have been drawn to work in many countries in the world, I have been able to see each country in a new way, the elements that we all have in common, and the elements that make a culture unique. I look for the art and music of a culture, the physical elements of the environment, the leaves and flowers, the animals and the attitudes toward animals, the flags, clothing, food, and architecture, the music, art, and dance, and the literary traditions. This is a mental checklist that I carry with me that helps me immediately appreciate each place where I travel.

There are many interesting stories about how students' lives were changed during these weeks. For myself I had become deeply involved with a leaf collection I was required to assemble during high school for a biology class. My mother arranged for me to spend an afternoon on the property of a local man who had been collecting trees from around the world for many years. He was very happy to share his stories of the hundreds of examples and to allow me to pick a leaf from each to mount in my collection with the scientific name and the local name. But during the leaf collection part of our filling-in-the-blanks weeks I discovered a way that I could share this passion with children. Giving a child the name of a tree to memorize just wouldn't do, but I learned that there were parts of the plant that a child could learn about and could recognize with his own eyes. For example if the shape of a leaf was "triangular" or "orbicular" it didn't matter if it was a tiny weed growing close to the ground, hidden under a large plant, or a very large leaf on a very large tree. The child could recognize it, name it, and go on to look for other examples. You will find in the leaf collection part of this book that there are many more keys to give a child so that he can explore with his own information.

Another example just given to me this week as I discussed this book with a friend, occurred during her own AMI primary training in Washington DC. At the end of a Friday lecture, her trainer said something like "How could you teach the children about art in Spain in the 14th Century if you don't know anything about art in Spain in the 14th Century?" The first thought of my friend, who was raised in a small town in the Midwest with no art museums was, "There was art in 14th century Spain?" She went on to spend many hours that year in the National Gallery enjoying art of all kinds from all over the world.

Over the years I have watched traditional, public and private, schools in the US gradually remove all the things that

I really enjoyed as a child such as nature walks, music and art, plays, concerts, being read great literature, dancing and so on. This was done in hopes that it would help the math and language scores go up. But language is no fun when it is taught only as a dry skill with nothing interesting to read and write about.

In the late 1970's I wrote a paper on Howard Gardner's Multiple Intelligences theory based on the book *Frames of Mind* as part of a Masters degree. Soon after that I was fortunate to take a class from him at Harvard Graduate School of Education. His idea was that there are mainly two kinds of intelligences that humans are born with that are valued and measured in our traditional system of education. These are verbal-linguistic and logical-mathematical, yep, language and math. These are easy to test and measure.

There are other intelligences and skills that have a lot to do with the happiness and success of the growing child and adult. He proposed eight, including the intelligence of music and rhythm, visual=spatial, body or kinesthetic, awareness of self (intrapersonal) and of others (interpersonal) and having a profound sense of nature (naturalist). A very good practical introduction to these ideas, combining clear explanations and practical advice in recognizing the special skills in children, can be found in the book *In Their Own Way: Discovering and Encouraging Your Child's Multiple Intelligences,* by Dr. Thomas Armstrong.

When we think of great people from the past do we only think of those people who were good at language and math? Or do we value the creators in all fields, people who are generous and help others, or the skills of getting along with others, helping groups work well together, making music or art or dance, creating through the use of imagination in both the arts and sciences, helping humanity? I think the latter. Language and math are essential! They give humans the tools to explore and express all of the other areas of knowledge, but they become dry and uninteresting when isolated from the rest of the world of knowledge.

What about happiness? One day, after that momentous and confusing trip around the world at age 20, I asked my parents what was the meaning, the purpose of life. Without batting an eye my father gave me an answer I never forgot. He did not say the purpose is to earn a lot of money, not fame, nor power. He said, "If at the end of each day if I have made life better in a small way for one person my life is worth living." He was right.

In Montessori, when the method of raising children is correctly followed, there is a melding of academic learning with the experience of happiness, happiness that comes from solving problems, meeting goals, satisfying curiosity, experiencing uninterrupted concentration, and from helping others.

I do hope that if you decide, as parents or teachers or educators in general, to start these collections that you enjoy having your eyes open to the world in all its beauty. If you share your new loves with children you will be giving a gift that will last a lifetime.

As Dr. Montessori says in *To Educate the Human Potential*:

The secret of good teaching is to regard the child's intelligence as a fertile field in which seeds may be sown, to grow under the heat of flaming imagination. Our aim is not only to make the child understand, and still less to force him to memorize, but so to touch his imagination as to enthuse him to his innermost core.

MIND THE GAPS

GENERAL KNOWLEDGE

The AMI 2.5-6 course I attended in London, England in 1970-1971 was an eye-opener in many ways. In the first weeks we combined learning about Montessori theory with filling in our own general knowledge by searching for information in the museums and gardens of the city. The following lists are from this assignment. Many of the pictures are from my own general knowledge album, or folder, created at that time. Almost fifty years later I still have my general knowledge album and enjoy sharing it with my grandchildren who, as Montessori students themselves can relate to this breadth of knowledge. I hope you enjoy gathering similar information for yourself, either as a parent or teacher, or just an outline for experiencing your world.

Wildflowers

The first picture shows the title page of the "wildflower" section of my general knowledge album. Working with students on the first AMI primary course in Morocco in 2018 I learned that, thanks to the Internet, it is much easier now to find pictures. However, there is a tendency to cut and paste the text rather than to read it and decide what to include in the album.

If you have no experience yet working with children, you can focus on information that is general and of interest to you. After you have experience working with children, however, you will find out what information, what interesting details, catch their attention and make them want to know more. That is our goal for all of the general knowledge areas, botany, zoology, history and geography, art, and music.

Botany

Find a picture and write a few paragraphs of interesting facts about six of each of the following: Garden flowers, Wildflowers, and Trees.

Create a title page for each of these three areas of botany. Give each example, each unique flower or tree, at least one full page. You might add more throughout the years, but this is the minimum.

Zoology

Find a picture and write a few paragraphs of interesting facts about six or more of each of the following:

Fish

Amphibians

Reptiles

Birds

Mammals

Birds

The order in which I have listed these classes of vertebrates, or animals with backbones, is not random. It follows the evolution of live on earth and will be studied in detail during the elementary, 6-12 years. Vertebrates are presented first, and so studied first by us adults, because these are the animals that are the easiest for children to see in detail. Invertebrates, animals without backbones such as insects, worms, sharks, and so on, will be studied later.

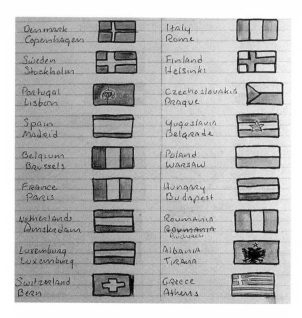

Denmark Copenhagen	Italy Rome	
Sweden Stockholm	Finland Helsinki	
Portugal Lisbon	Czechoslovakia Praque	
Spain Madrid	Yugoslavia Belgrade	
Belgium Brussels	Poland Warsaw	
France Paris	Hungary Budapest	
Netherlands Amsterdam	Roumania Roumania Bucharest	
Luxemburg Luxemburg	Albania Tirana	
Switzerland Bern	Greece Athens	

Geography 1, Continents

To begin the study of geography we research and record the names of the countries, the capitals, and the flags, of each of the six continents that are vastly populated by humans: Africa, Asia, Australasia, Europe, North America, and South America (not Antarctica).

For example in the "Africa" section you will list each country, that county's capital and that country's flag. It is easy to find the flags on the Internet, but you will not learn that way. When working with the puzzle maps and flags in the Montessori class you will be teaching these names, and your general knowledge work is where you can begin to learn the vocabulary. You can see that the drawing in the above picture, from my own album, are simple color pencil sketches, but that little bit of work was enough to get me started learning the names.

The assignment I gave the students in Morocco was to do their own continent and a second continent that would be valuable for the children they will be working with. But at least one student went on to research and list the names of the countries and capitals, and draw the flags, for all six continents.

Geography 2, Countries

Choose one country from each continent that you would like to learn more about, six countries. Write a page or more about each country, including a drawing of the flag and at least one picture.

Include at least four other pictures for each country. Keep in mind the importance of pictures showing the physical needs of humans — food, clothing, transportation, shelter — but you can also include other elements unique to the country.

Keep these pictures in six plastic sheets to use when teaching, later adding more countries, perhaps when you visit one.

Geography 3, Land and Water Formations

These include island, lake, isthmus, strait, cape, bay, peninsula, and gulf.

Make a very simple drawing of each of these, water blue and land green or brown, and record the definitions in your album. Notice that these come in pairs, the island is the reverse of the lake, the isthmus is the reverse of the strait, and so on. Reflect this in your drawings.

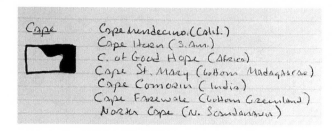

Cape

Cape Mendecino. (Calif.)
Cape Horn (S. Am.)
C. of Good Hope (Africa)
Cape St. Mary (bottom Madagascar)
Cape Comorin (India)
Cape Farewale (bottom Greenland)
North Cape (N. Scandanavia)

Island – a piece of land surrounded by water

Lake – a large body of water surrounded by land

Isthmus – a narrow strip of land with sea on either side, forming a link between two larger areas of land

Strait – a narrow passage of water connecting two seas or two other large areas of water

Cape – a point or extension of land jutting out into water as a peninsula or as a projecting point

Bay – a broad inlet of the sea where the land curves inward

Peninsula – a piece of land almost surrounded by water or projecting out into a body of water

Gulf - a deep inlet of the sea almost surrounded by land, with a narrow mouth

Using a world map or a globe (or the internet as a last resort) find and record the names of six of each of the land and water formations somewhere in the world. You can find examples from all 7 continents rather than 6. Notice this in the above picture.

Example 1:

Next to "island" you will have a drawing of an island, the definition of "island", and six examples from the world map.

Example 2:

Bass Strait (between Australia and Tasmania)

Cape of Good Hope (Africa)

Scientists

History - Biography

Research, find a picture, and gather interesting information for at least five of each of each of these groups: Poets, Composers or Musicians, Artists, Scientists and inventors, Authors

In your selection be sure to represent several centuries and places on earth. Of course be sure to include women in each group. When possible try to find a picture of his/her invention or creative work. Write a page or more about each person and include picture(s). Your text should include interesting incidents that can be used to tell little stories to children, facts about the person's childhood, talent, life, interests, family, etc. This is one of the most difficult subjects to make come alive for children because it is sometimes difficult to find information of interest to children, not just for adults. Sometimes there are very good books written just for young children that are a great help in this area, for text and pictures.

Art Cards General

Begin an art postcard collection showing paintings, sculpture, or drawings that are internationally recognizable. In

London we did this by going to museums. Do this if possible because that way you will see the originals before selecting postcards in the museum shop that are meaningful to you. Collect two identical postcards when possible for language lessons. The picture above shows the famous image of the Mona Lisa by Leonardo da Vinci. The layout is called the "identical matching" and is discussed in detail in the Language chapter.

As I mentioned above, as you begin to collect cards that you might use in the classroom, think about what details of the art or the artist will be interesting to children. For example in this image you could look for different colors, a green sky for example, and the fact that the woman seems to be looking right at us. The painting (show the size with your arms) was once owned by the king of France and now is in a museum in France; tell how many people look at it each year; "Mona" means "ma'am" or "Miss" or "Mrs. So the name is Miss Lisa; the artist was asked to paint this picture of a man's wife to celebrate the birth of their second son. Examine the background, the imaginary landscape of mountains, paths, a bridge, which was a new feature in portraits at this time.

If you have Leonardo da Vinci as one of the examples of artists in your biography section, think about these same kinds of details that might interest a child, not an adult student of art history.

As in all areas of Montessori we start with the big picture and make our way to the details, so with art cards we begin with the general collection, then art of continents, then art of countries in the students own continent, then the art of the students country, then individual artists, and finally the details in art works.

Art Cards by Continent

For this assignment, collect postcards of pictures of art from each of the six continents where many humans live and where there is a tradition of art. These include: Asia, Africa, N. America, S. America, Europe, and Australia.

For the Morocco course, I assigned students to create six sets with at least two images in each. Some of the students wanted to find more than two examples and I encourage you to do the same.

Art Cards by Country

Collect postcards of pictures of the art of your own country first and then other countries. In Morocco our assignment was at least four countries, with each set containing at least two images.

Art Cards of Individual Artists

First, collect postcards of pictures of the artist you love, then branch out to learn to appreciate other kinds of art. Two-dimensional art such as images of paintings are very good because they can be found in many books on art, but you can also include images of photographs and famous sculptures. Above you see two pieces of sculpture by August Rodin. This art is especially meaningful to me because long ago when I studied in Paris each day I walked past a garden filled with his sculptures, and "The Thinker" sculpture can be seen at the Legion of Honor in San Francisco, one of my favorite art museums. Also I have found that this sculpture of hands is always interesting to children as they imagine making a sculpture of something as simple as a person's hands.

Our official, very minimum, assignment was at least three artists, each set containing at least two images.

Art Cards of Details in Art

After children see these things in classroom art card collections, they are likely to spend a lot more time and attention looking at art in books. One of the most successful museum visits for children is to look for one detail in many pieces of art, paintings or sculptures. Examples of details to look for are unlimited but could include feet, food, children, flowers (as in the image above), skies, toys, animals, etc. They will be able to look for these details in books and in museums, giving a focus for exploring art.

The assignment was at least four categories, three pictures each.

Music

Music was not part of our general knowledge album but filling in the gaps in our music education is a pleasurable task and I have helped many teachers bring this area to the classroom. You might include the music of composers you have researched in the History-Biography section of your general knowledge album.

The layout of the picture of Johann Sebastian Bach above is called the "three-part cards" and is discussed in the Language chapter

Indigenous music is sometimes becoming difficult to find as our world becomes more and more homogenous, but children are very sensitive to the variety of music of other cultures and this is the time to introduce it. I suggest that you find a CD (or whatever the technology is as you read this book) for each of the two areas of music below.

Cultural Music

Asia - pick a country in Asia that you want to learn more about.

Africa - pick a country in Africa that you want to learn more about.

North America – be sure to include Native American flute music

South America – pick a country you want to learn more about. For myself I love the traditional music of the Andean mountains.

Australia – the didgeridoo music of the Australian Aborigines is fascinating

Europe - pick a country in Europe that you want to learn more about.

Western Classical Music

Find a CD of music for each of these time divisions of Western music:

Baroque (1600–1750)

Classical (1750–1820)

Romantic (1810–1910)

Impressionist (1875-1925)

Postmodern or *Contemporary* (1930-present)

It might seem that Western classical music is just western, but everywhere I travel I hear the same wonderful sounds of Chopin, Bach, and so on. This shows that this music came from a place that resonates with people through out the ages and all over the earth, and it will be the same for us and for the children in our lives.

MIND THE GAPS

LEAF COLLECTION

In 2018 I gave a presentation of leaves similar to what you find in this chapter and then led a nature walk with the students in the AMI primary course in Casablanca, Morocco, in a beautiful garden in the home of my hosts. The students were hesitant at first, but very quickly found themselves as excited as children as they discovered the ways that the leaves were attached to the stems—alternately, oppositely, or whorled or in a group of leaves all attached at the same point. And one student noticed that the leaves that have veins that are parallel tend to have smooth margins (edge of the leaf), so she set off to find an exception to this "rule."

As we prepared to leave the garden and headed down the path toward the vehicles, I noticed several of the students walking slowly, looking carefully, and taking pictures. This is just the kind of involvement we will see in our children when we share the desire to explore and learn more with them.

Exploring the local environment and creating one's own leaf album was one of the most interesting and enjoyable parts of my first Montessori diploma course. It opened my eyes to botany in a way I had never expected. Because of this first introduction I believe I was much more successful than I would have been in inspiring children to become aware of the fascinating world of plants. It enabled me to understand and share the names and properties of leaves, their margins, the attachments to stems and other properties, and inspired me to create all of the language materials to which I have referred to above.

I remember the story of a friend who took the London course years before I did. One day during the early weeks of the course she was all dressed up and taking a break from the course work to meet a friend for lunch in the center of London. Now this was a very elegant and beautiful lady and I am sure many eyes were turned in her direction as she headed for her meeting. Suddenly she glanced at a tree branch above her, stopped in her tracks and exclaimed, "A Palmately compound leaf!" She later said with a gleam in her eye as she told me the story, "I always wondered what people on the sidewalk who witnessed this strange behavior must have thought."

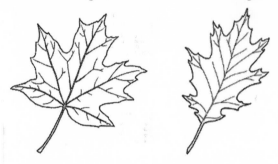

The same excitement still overtakes me at times. Once, on a long drive from San Francisco to home with my husband we pulled over at a rest area park to take a little walk. Of course I was looking up into the trees. Excitedly I picked one leaf from a maple tree and another from an oak and pointed out to my husband how both were *fid* (the distance from the margin to the center of the leaf) but one was *palmately fid* (the maple) and the other *pinnately fid*. And didn't he think that this was interesting? He is used to this kind of excitement over discoveries by now and indeed agreed with me.

If you are a parent or teacher of any kind I recommend that you create a leaf album and discover the excitement I am talking about. When you have learned to see the world in this new way, to explore as you look for a particular specimen, and to take delight in discovery of the variety, you will be on your way to sharing these interests with your children or students.

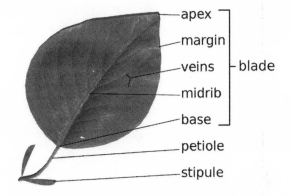

Here is a labeled picture of the parts of a leaf. This helps us make sense of the terms used below in describing the fascinating differences between the shapes of leaves.

CREATING THE LEAF COLLECTION

Leaf Album Introduction

Why do we give children the classification of leaves? First of all we are feeding the mental hunger of the child during the period of the absorbent mind. We are trying to give him a sense of wonder concerning nature that will arouse his interest and widen his scope, so he won't take these things for granted. The child is having many, many experiences at this age and a system of identifying things in nature, such as leaves, will help him to classify his experiences and to communicate about them. We are inspiring him to explore his world and to make order of it.

There are many systems of botany classification in the world. We use this particular classification, such as the way a leaf is attached to the stem of the plant, because these examples are very easy for the child to observe.

We give classification by the shapes of the leaves, such as *linear, ovate* and *triangular*, for several reasons:

These shapes are the basis for geometry. When the child comes to the study of geometric shapes he will already have had an interesting, living introduction to the shapes with which geometry deals.

These shapes are found throughout the natural and man-made world, for example the shape of the moon, of mineral crystals, of sculptures, and in architecture. Being already familiar with the shapes will help the child to see so much more in the world, to see as an artist sees, helping him understand the interrelatedness of all things.

A classification by shapes such as *elliptical* and *orbiculate* instead of scientific or arbitrary local names such as *maple* or *elm* will help the child abstract the concept and think for himself.

The common name can be a problem. For example the Sansevieria plant was named after Prince of San Seviero by the Swedish naturalist Carl Thunberg, and it is also called snake plant, mother-in-law's tongue, viper's bowstring hemp, and Saint George's sword, depending on where one lives. And it has two different leaf shapes on the same plant so the child can use his own information in naming the leaf. And the Sassafras tree has three different shapes of leaves on the same plant— and a child can name them all by shape! He will be able to classify leaves wherever he is and from his own knowledge instead of accepting the classification from someone else.

If one researches the classification of leaves and leaf attachment to the stem one will find conflicting systems. It is not the case that one system is right and one is wrong, but if we all use the one that has been used in Montessori classrooms for many years a child is prepared when a family relocates and he joins another class.

Leaves can be tiny weeds, large leaves on bushes and trees, or garden plants. Many specimens can be found growing in the most unexpected places such as very close to the ground hidden by larger plants, or even pushing their way through cracks in a city sidewalk or parking lot.

For my album I dried the leaves between the pages of a newspaper and then, placing one leaf per page with the label handwritten at the bottom of the page covered the leaf with a piece of plastic, the kind today used to protect book covers in libraries and schools. Be sure your leaves are completely dry before placing them on an album page and covering with plastic.

This is the list I used for the Table of Contents at the beginning of my leaf album:

1 – *Introduction* (given above)

2 - *Phyllotaxis* (the leaf attachment to the stem)

3 - *Veins* (parallel and reticulate)

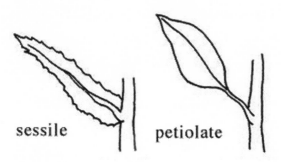

sessile   petiolate

Phyllotaxis

The term Phyllotaxis refers to the attachment of the leaf to the stem. The term is from Ancient Greek *phýllon* "leaf" and *táxis* "arrangement". There are two main classifications.

Phyllotaxis classification I:

Petiolate – leaf connected to the stem of the plant by a simple petiole

Sessile – leaf connected directly to the stem without a petiole

Phyllotaxis classification 2:

Alternate – the leaves are attached to the stem alternating from one to the next

Opposite – pairs of leaves are attached at the same place on the stem

Whorled – more than two leaves attached to the stem in a group

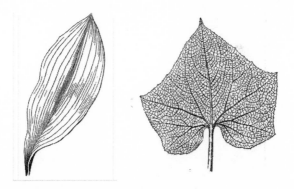

Leaf Veins, Venation

Parallel, veins parallel to each other

Reticulate, netlike

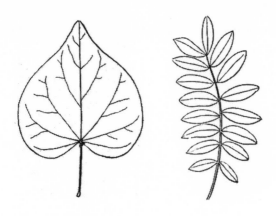

Simple and Compound Leaves

Simple means there is only one leaf, one leaf blade.

Compound refers to one leaf that contains more than one leaflet. The leaflets of a compound leaf will not have a petiole. A leaf may or may not.

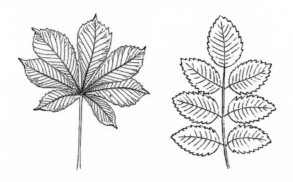

Palmately and pinnately compound leaves

There are two main kinds of compound leaves:

Palmately compound, leaflets attached to the tip of the petiole, similar to fingers reaching out from the *palm* of the hand

Pinnately compound, pairs of leaflets attached opposite to each other along an extension of the petiole, which it helps me to think of as a *pin*

Margins

Entire – smooth, without indentations or incisions on margins

Dented – not smooth but with small indentations

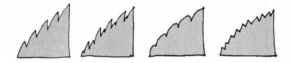

Four types of dented margins

Serrate - with pointed teeth pointing toward the apex of the leaf

Bi-serrate - smaller and larger teeth alternate

Crenate - round-toothed with the teeth cut less than 1/8 way to midvein.

Dentate - with rounded or sharp, coarse teeth that point outwards at right angles to midvein, cut 1/16 to 1/8 distance to midvein.

Margin Character

The character of the leaf margin refers to the distance between the edge of the blade, the *margin*, and the petiole or midvein.

Just as with the palmate and pinnate classification of the compound leaves, palmate and pinnate are used in describing the margin character.

Palmately lobed - round-toothed, cut in 1/8-1/4 of the distance to petiole

Palmately fid - having lobes with incisions that extend less than halfway toward the petiole

Palmately partite - having lobes with incisions that extend over halfway toward the petiole

Palmately sect - Having lobes with incisions that extend almost up, but not quite to the petiole.

Pinnately lobed - round-toothed, cut 1/8-1/4 distance to midvein

Pinnately fid - having lobes with incisions that extend less than halfway toward the midvein

Pinnately partite – having lobes with incisions that extend over halfway toward the midvein

Pinnately sect - having lobes with incisions that extend almost up, but not quite to the midvein

Margin by Geometric Shapes

Some of these shapes are found in the leaf cabinet and will be referred to later, in the botany chapter of this book.

PELTATE

Here is a picture of my own leaf collection title page and the page displaying an actual dried peltate leaf. This album was created in London during the course in 1970. The leaves were pressed between newspapers, weighted down by heavy books, and then attached to the page with the kind of clear plastic used to protect book covers. Imagine, almost 50 years later I was able to take this picture for you! My children, grandchildren, students, and other young friends have enjoyed looking at this collection over the years.

Aciculate – needle-shaped as in pine

Hastate – shaped like an arrowhead with the two basal lobes, near the petiole, directed outwards

Cordate – heart-shaped, petiole attached at the notch or indentation

Obcordate – heart-shaped, petiole attached at the tapering end

Elliptical – like an ellipse, generally symmetrical, elongated, and more or less evenly rounded at both ends

Ensiform – sword shaped

Lanceolate - shaped like a lance, wider in the middle or near the petiole

Oblanceolate – shaped like a lance, with the widest portion near the tip or apex, the reverse of lanceolate

Linear – many times longer than broad, approximately parallel sides

Lyrate – shaped like a lyre, a pinnately lobed leaf with an enlarged terminal lobe and smaller lateral lobes

Orbiculate – round

Peltate – a round leaf where the petiole attaches near the center of the blade

Ovate – oval, egg-shaped, with the widest portion near the petiole

Obovate – oval, egg-shaped, with the widest portion near the apex, reverse of ovate, opposite of ovate

Reniform – kidney-shaped — an oval with an inward curve on one side, at the base

Runcinate – having incised margins with the lobes or teeth curved toward the base or Petiole, directed away from the apex or tip of the leaf

Sagittate – shaped like an arrowhead with the lower lobes pointing or curled downward

Spatulate – Spoon-shaped, having a broad flat end that tapers to the base, near the petiole

Triangulate – triangle shaped

RENIFORM   RUNCINATE

Here you can see examples of both a reniform and runcinate leaf from my album.

WORKING WITH CHILDREN

When you are sharing these discoveries with children be sure to focus on only one classification at a time, either with plants in the classroom or on a nature walk. If you are going for a walk be sure to explore ahead of time so there will be satisfying discoveries.

Keep it simple and clear, just looking for one type of classification at first. For example you might look for sessile and petiolate attachments to the stem of the plant. Another day look for leaf margins that are entire (smooth) and those that are dented. Another day look for simple and compound leaves. There is no rush and the purpose is not to cover the complete curriculum, but to open one's eyes to the amazing beauty and variety in the world of leaves and to inspire more exploration.

We always give the real example, as many varieties as possible, before giving the language. The saying is, "Sensorial before language." Which means the child must be exposed to several examples of a thing and begin to abstract the concept. At this point the label or language has meaning.

You can have a leaf press in the classroom, and use leaves for printmaking. Many children will want to draw and label their leaves.

Some of the leaves that I found for my album were tiny and some were large. I loved walking around London focusing on the gardens and the tiny weeds sticking their tiny bodies up through the cracks in the pavement. Some were very difficult to find but that was not an obstacle to completing the album as we all helped each other by coming back to class and telling fellow students where to go to find a particular example.

LYRATE

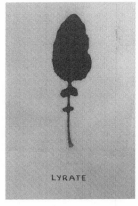
LYRATE

Here are two different examples, from different plants, of the lyrate leaf. Sometimes I just couldn't stop and so there were several leaves of the same kind in the album. If you decide to make an album for yourself I hope you have the same experience because it is just this unquenchable curiosity that brings all subject to life, and the children will see it in your face and hear it in your voice when you share your work.

MIND THE GAPS

FORMAL LANGUAGE BOOK

During the first six years of life the development of language is very well supported in Montessori environments. The child is listened to and given the vocabulary of his environment, food, clothing, friends, colors, sounds, materials, everything he can see and touch. But there is more.

Formal language refers to the language of song and poetry, of traditions of language reaching back through time and across the world. It expands the everyday, informal, language that the child hears every day at home and in the Montessori environment.

The song, "Twinkle, Twinkle, Little Star" is formal language. A child does not yet know what the word *twinkle* means even though he might know what the words *little* and *star* mean. In the first part of William Blake's poem "The Tyger" (one of the children's favorites in my primary classes) "TYGER BURNING BRIGHT; In the forests of the night; What immortal hand or eye; Could frame thy fearful symmetry?" a child might recognize the words *tiger, burning, forests, hand, eye*, or more, but he will love learning the whole piece because of the fascinating sounds and rhythm.

But as he grows, he will pay attention to all of the other words he learns in this way and gradually abstract the meanings.

Another example is the action rhyme, "Jack be nimble, Jack be quick; Jack jump over the candlestick." In my class we had an old-fashioned candleholder, a "candlestick" with a little handle that was used for walking on the line (walking so slowly that the flame was not extinguished). Sometimes a child would place the candlestick on the floor and jump over it when he came to the word *jump* while reciting the nursery rhyme. Learning finger plays and action rhymes makes the meaning and use of verbs clear to the child.

I wrote out many of the poems in my collection on cards, drawing a little picture at the top, and kept them standing upright in a wooden box in the classroom. A child who could not yet read could find the poem or rhyme or song or finger play he wanted to hear because of the little pictures at the top and then take the card to a friend to read or sing it. My oldest daughter made the cards in this picture during her own primary training in London.

We all have cherished memories of certain songs and nursery rhymes, etc., that we want to share with children, and learning more is as enjoyable for us as for our children. My own collection was kept in my classroom and later used with children and grandchildren, and I added to it regularly, especially when someone taught me new guitar chords for songs I wanted to be able to sing.

When making your personal collection here are some things to keep in mind.

The formal language collection should contain a range of subjects of interest to children, drawing on the whole world of plants, animals, and people, and should contain as much for the 4-6 year old as for the 2.5 to 3 year old. As many languages as possible can be represented as long as you can model the correct pronunciation.

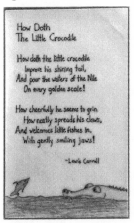

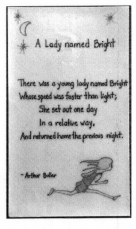

The formal language collection can be divided into the following categories: poems, nursery rhymes, songs, singing games, finger plays, and action rhymes

In my own book I added a section for "stories" to keep track of favorite simple stories my children loved to hear about my own experiences, such as the time our horse got out of the paddock and looked in at the window at us one morning as we were having breakfast!

What is the difference between a nursery rhyme and a poem? A nursery rhyme is part of the tradition of literature for children in a culture and usually rhymes. A poem is a piece of writing that may or may not rhyme. It may have a more complicated structure and may convey a more complicated message or meaning. All poems must be attributed to an author or a source "unknown."

What is the difference between a song and a singing game? One person can sing a song anytime. A singing game involves singing in a group and it involves whole body movements.

What is the difference between a finger play and an action rhyme? A finger play includes specific uses of the fingers and an action rhyme involves other body movements.

Can one example fit into more than one category? Yes, there are many favorite nursery rhymes, "Baa, baa, black sheep" for example, that are sometimes recited and sometimes sung. It is up to you where you want to keep each example.

If your book will be available in the classroom for children to see, you should be sure that everything is spelled correctly and that you have taken care to create a beautiful book to share with the children.

If your children are learning to write in cursive, then the book should be carefully written in cursive. If they are learning Italics, write it in Italics. It definitely should not be printed out from a computer or written in all capital letters.

When growing your anthology look for poems and songs appropriate for special celebrations and times of the year.

THE FORMAL LANGUAGE ASSIGNMENT

Here is the assignment I gave to the students in the primary course in Morocco:

To begin, create an album, with a lovely title page, and title pages for the tabbed sections:

5 poems

5 nursery rhymes

5 songs

5 singing games

5 finger plays

5 action rhymes

Diggory Diggory Delvet

Diggory Diggory Delvet!
A little old man in black
velvet;

He digs and he delves —
You can see for yourselves
The mounds dug by
Diggory Delvet.

The
Caterpillar

Brown and furry
Caterpillar in a hurry;
Take your walk
To the shady leaf,
or stalk.

May no toad spy on you,
May the little bird pass by you;
Spin and die,
To live again a butterfly.

- Christina Rossetti

It is one of the greatest discoveries in the power of language when a young child realizes that a particular favorite card, when taken to any friend or adult who can read, will always result in the same poem being read. It is like magic!

Since the poems on the cards are beautifully written sometimes an older child will choose one and carefully copy the text and illustrations to make his own poetry cards.

This is the plan for filling in the gaps in the adult's education. In the next chapters we will see ideas for how to share our world with children.

INTRODUCTION
TO THE CULTURE ALBUM

D r. Montessori described education as "a help to life". We must help the child, above all, to adapt to his time and place in history and in the world, and to be oriented to his group. This adaptation, in the widest sense of the word, means to become his own person, an educated and valuable member of a family, a country, the world, and the universe. That is the reason that we offer as wide a cultural basis as possible, in the fields of physics, biology, geography, history, and the arts.

In the first three years of life the child has already begun to absorb, or take in without effort, the attitude toward these areas in his daily life. This way of learning continues through age six. From birth to age six the child takes in all impressions effortlessly and completely, and these impressions become part of him, forming his mind. Things that the child experiences at this age, elements of the world to which he is exposed now, become very special to him later in life. We can help him then to make contact, now, with both the natural and the man-made world in ways that are appropriate to his stage of development.

Because we cannot give the child the whole world we give him "keys" that open the doors to the world, inspiring his own exploration now and in the future. Through these key experiences we instill an interest in, and a respect for, the inanimate world of physics such as water and air, and also plants, animals, and human beings in his own culture and the cultures of the world.

How do we provide a rich environment for this broad cultural basis? There will be a lot of information on how to do this as we delve deeper into each area, but here is a broad explanation for us to begin to think about our work. We prepare a rich environment in which the child is free to explore all of these areas according to his needs and interests.

PRACTICAL LIFE

We give him appropriate practical life exercises related to each subject to help him make use of the best possible contact with these subjects by working in and on his environment. These provide techniques for both physical and mental exploration.

SENSORIAL KEYS

Whatever we give the child it must fulfill the needs of the motor-sensorial period, which is a characteristic of this stage of development. We do not ask the child to sit still while we "teach" him, or educate the intellect about these things, but we provide a means by which the child can learn through movement and through his senses, from which his intellect if formed.

We provide and present to the child sensorial keys to each part of the environment. It is most important that the directress is interested in, somewhat knowledgeable about, and continuing to learn about, these subjects in order to interest the child. These sensorial keys provide the means for him to initiate his own experiences in these fields, they provide the opportunity for repetition which is necessary for learning, and they inspire him to go forward with his explorations, now and later in life.

LANGUAGE

First we give the experiences, and when these are solid we provide the correct and exact language so that the child can classify his experiences and talk about them, thereby fulfilling his need for communication.

HANDWORK

Last of all we provide handwork, artwork, and further activities so that he can further process, becomes aware of, and apply his knowledge. In this way he begins to see the interrelationship of the various cultural subjects, for example combining the world of plants with art by making leaf prints.

THE ENVIRONMENT

A child's reaction to the environment is his own creation according to his experiences. His life can be enriched or thwarted according to his environment. But because today's world is so very complex and fast-paced, we must more than ever, think of the children's house environment as a peaceful and simple one, adapted to the needs of the child.

In the first *casa dei bambini* in Italy more than a hundred years ago Maria Montessori observed children at length and adapted the environment according to what she learned from watching them. She provided equipment and taught children how to wash their own hands thoroughly, to clean their nose, to care for themselves without help, in the first practical life exercises.

At first the adult helper handed out the materials until Montessori realized that children liked to pick out their own equipment, and to put it away on their own, and that their choices could be trusted. She learned that the children had a natural tendency toward keeping things in order. Reading and writing also became a part of this first prepared environment as she discovered that the children enjoyed learning the letters. The children, with the aid of this first prepared environment, became independent personalities, quiet, kind, hardworking, and ordered.

Below are some general principles for preparing the environment of cultural area of the primary class.

The Room

The classroom itself should be well built, fitting the country in which it is found. The windows should be low so that the children can see out. Places should be available where the children can tend plants. In Colombia, South America both of the schools I visited all had 3-walled classrooms because the climate was hot and being open to the air provided relief from the heat. It also exposed the world of nature to the children at all ages.

Doors

Door handles should be low. Some schools have no doors but a series of classrooms where children at different levels are free to visit other classes.

The Floor

The floor should be clean, polished, with little felt mats, floor mats, that are stored in one place and the children able to access them at any time. Then the children learn to brush them and put them away, sometimes rolling them up, when they are finished. Avoid carpets so spilling is not a problem. And avoid large rugs that in traditional classrooms would be used for whole-class, large group lessons. These are not found in Montessori classrooms except in rare exceptions.

Stairs

Steps or stairs are good to have so children practice walking and carrying things on them.

Furniture

Furniture should be fitted to the sizes of the children in the group so that their feet can be flat on the floor and the body balanced. Stools rather than chairs are very good for this purpose. An armchair, like one used by adults, is nice to have in the book corner. All furniture should be of the best quality available, wood rather than plastic, and kept in perfect condition. When this is the case the children themselves will be drawn to take care of and to clean them.

Lighting

Natural lighting from windows or a free flow to an inside-outside classroom environment whenever possible is excellent. For inside lighting research can tell us, as things change, which light bulbs are healthy for humans. Table lamps give a feeling of a child's home rather than a classroom.

Tables and Chairs

For many reasons wood tables and chairs are best. Also wood of a light shade is best so dirt will show and the children can see that they need to clean them. Pay attention to the weight, not so light that they will tip over, but light enough so that children can easily carry them independently. Since protecting concentration is of highest priority it is best to have one-person tables rather than tables for two children or larger tables for groups that are found in non-Montessori environments. Many children will choose to work at a single table facing the wall with a framed piece of art in front of him and no visual distraction.

Cupboards and Shelves

These should be low and open in front, the right size to keep the material in a neat and not over-crowded way so the children are drawn to it. There should be a place for everything so that the children always know where to put things back.

Pegs or Hooks

These should be at a level convenient for the children to easily hang up their own coats or bags holding inside shoes if that is appropriate for your climate. Since dressing and undressing are important practical life activities, these should be in or near the classroom so the teacher can give the lessons, rather than having parents dress and undress children,

A Mirror

Hung in the dressing/undressing area this mirror should be of a size and shape that allows a child to see his whole body and check on his own to see that he is clean and neat. Having tissue and a wastebasket near by allows him to care for his nose and face.

Decorations

Art should be hung at the child's eye level and nothing above it at the adult eye level. In an art gallery for adults a painting, for example, is hung so that the center of the painting is at the adult's eye level. The art should represent the very best of visual art, or realistic and attractive pictures of the subjects of culture, animals, plant, people, musical instruments, and so on. There should not be anything hung above this level.

Teaching Materials

The teaching materials or equipment should be made of wood, glass, metal, stone, etc., rather than plastic whenever possible. It should be clean and kept in as perfect condition as possible, and kept very neatly on the shelves. The adult is the model and the children will follow her lead, as a sense of order is natural in children at this age. If there is a chip in the paint that material should be removed and repaired before it is returned to the classroom.

Cultural Areas

Just as with the other areas of the Montessori primary environment, each cultural area should be distinct in the physical environment in order to be sure that all areas are kept rich and interesting on their own. For example all of the physics experiments are kept together, the art materials are kept together, the botany the same, and so on. This keeps each area present visually and leads to a child's understanding that the world has many elements of equal importance.

Table mats and floor mats

These tools are very important in aiding concentration. A child might decide what he wants to work on. The first step is for him to decide if this is best done on a table or the floor. Then he places a tablemat or a floor mat in the space he is planning to work, and then gathers the materials. All this is part of the logical process of work that is so valuable for keeping the child focused and thinking. The work cycle comes to an end as the child folds and puts away the tablemat, or rolls up the floor mat and puts it away. These mats should be of a solid color to help the focus be on the material. Have many floor mats because working on the floor helps a child concentrate on work, and sitting on the floor is good for the body.

Teachers Space

There is no teacher's desk in a children's house, and all of the directress' materials should be stored out of sight of the children. It is important that the children see adults writing with pencils and not on computers so I recommend that teachers record their observations by pencil in the classroom and anything stored on a computer is done out of the sight of children.

Concrete First and then Abstraction

We give the experience of the real object first. For example we might have a pet rabbit visit the classroom and show the child the feet, the nose, the mouth, and so on, before we would introduce pictures of rabbits and other mammals, or language cards used to teach the exterior parts of mammals.

The Whole and then the Parts

We give the whole and then work our way to the details. For example the land and water globe, next the continent puzzle maps, then the puzzle map of the countries of the child's continent, and then the puzzle map of the states or territories of the child's country.

Ideology

In our minds we always remember that we are helping to shape a citizen of the world first and foremost, presenting a global oneness where the differences should be enjoyed for the richness it brings to life.

Limited Experience

We give enough to spark an interest, but not so much as to overwhelm a child. There is a saying, "The adult is in charge of the minimum, the child the maximum." It is better to have a child wanting more than wanting a break from work!

Human Tendencies

A child has a need or tendency to be curious, to explore, and to orient himself in his environment in preparation for doing the same later in the wider world. At this age he has a need to move, to speak, and to repeat over and over what he is working on. When we give a lesson we always invite the child to repeat, but we do not require it.

Sensitive Periods

We keep in mind the sensitive periods, such as for language and for order, order in where things are kept as well as order for what comes next during the day.

Control of Error

There should always be some kind of control of error that the child can see in order to help him be independent in work, not needing to come and ask an adult if the work has been done correctly. For example in doing a puzzle map of the continents it is clear to the child, without needing the adult, when all of the pieces have been placed correctly. The three-part language cards are very good examples of good control of error. More on this can be found on the chapter on language.

Inviting to the Lesson

The child is always invited to a lesson not told what to do. He must feel that the choice is his. At the end of the lesson the teacher invites the child to repeat saying to come and get her when he is finished so she can show him the end of the lesson. Children at this age usually can only focus on listening or watching so the teacher is careful to stop talking when she wants the child to watch what she is doing. A lesson is not complete until the child has been shown how to put everything back in perfect condition for the next child to get out. This gives the child a way to contribute to the group, a first social activity.

1:1 Lessons

There are times when a lesson might be given to more than one child at a time. For example when beginning a new class the teacher has group lessons all day long as children learn how to run the class by themselves. In a normalized class if there are a few new children they will need group lessons for the same reason. Group lessons are also given when there are a few children who just haven't been able to settle to work on their own, and in the elementary class for the five great lessons at the beginning of the year. The rest of the time the lessons are given to one child at a time. If another child wants to watch he or she is taught how to watch without interrupting, just as they are taught not to interrupt any child working at any time.

As Montessori said, in her book *The Absorbent Mind*, about a child having been shown new lessons:

> When the child begins to show interest in one of these, the teacher must not interrupt, because this interest corresponds with natural laws and opens up a whole cycle of new activities. But the first step is so fragile, so delicate, that a touch can make it vanish again, like a soap bubble, and with it goes all the beauty of that moment.

Free Choice

A child is free at any time during the day (afternoons as well as mornings) to make his own choice of any work he understands how to use, or we might say, "Any material he has had a lesson on." But having a lesson doesn't always mean he has had a formal lesson by the teacher. He could have had a lesson from another child, or by carefully watching another child. It is the skill of the teacher to know when the use of the materials is productive. The child should be free to choose his own work because this is the only way he will be able to use his own intelligence to explore, experiment, and master everything he wants to master.

The adult always practices lessons on her own, or by giving them to another adult, before giving them to a child. This helps one discover if the materials work well, and enables one to isolate any difficulties so the presentation is as clear and logical as possible.

All of the above refers to the physical environment of the child. Though it is very important, it must be combined with an environment emotionally and spiritually prepared as well in order to be effective. The child must have love and security and respect for his person and his choices and ideas — and an attitude that will stimulate his interests, aid him in becoming physically and mentally independent, and serve as a model for how he will treat others.

Just as with the practical life, sensorial, language, and math work, the cultural lessons are not given by lectures of an adult, but they are given to one child at a time. You will see that each area — physics, biology, history and geography, and the arts—has a practical life area where a child learns to care for and respect the materials. Each area has a sensorial area, which heightens the experience through as many senses as possible. Each area has specific lessons to isolate principles. And each area has specific language, which helps to abstract these principles and gives the child the tools to communicate, through speaking and writing and reading, about each area.

Each lesson can inspire wonder, help the child want to know more, and lead to deep concentration, then happiness and kindness, which is the main goal of our work.

> *When the children had completed an absorbing bit of work, they appeared rested and deeply pleased. It almost seemed as if a road had opened up within their souls that led to all their latent powers, revealing the better part of themselves. They exhibited a great affability to everyone, put themselves out to help others and seemed full of good will. Then it would happen that one of them would quietly approach the teacher and whisper to her, as if confiding a great secret, "I'm a good boy!"*
>
> —Montessori, *Child in the Family*

THE WORLD OF PHYSICS

The goal of scientific pursuit should not merely be to make use of the world around us. It should be to understand it, fundamentally. No matter what use it might be. From the smallest molecule to the largest galaxy.

— Albert Einstein

Physics is the study of the mechanics of why matter or physical objects react in a particular way. Children experience physics since birth as they discover the movement of leaves in a tree caused by the wind, play in sand and water and mud, and lift heavy objects, or examine rocks with a magnifying glass. After age 6, in the elementary class and beyond, they will study matter at a molecular level; this study is called *chemistry*.

The reason we give this work to the young child is to give experience with isolated examples of the natural principles of physics in everyday life. Physical laws apply everywhere and every time. This is an introduction to real life, to truth, rather than opinion and belief. Science thrives on the universality of physical laws and just as we give "keys" to the worlds of color, shape, size, smell, etc., with the sensorial materials, we give keys to the experiences of electricity, shadows, magnetic attraction, the characteristics of air and water, heat, sound, light, and more, to help the child explore, orient himself, and classify his environment. Curiosity and science in general thrive on the universality of these physical laws.

At this age we use mostly everyday equipment, things that can be found in everyday life, not specifically scientific equipment. There should be only one experiment for one principle. Each experiment should contain a sensorial "key" to a basic physical law, not just an amusing trick.

The experiments introduce experiences with buoyancy (an object sinking or floating), the movement of water, surface tension of water, movement of air, heat, sound, magnetism, electricity, gravity, weight combined with movement, and weight affected by shape.

PREPARING THE ENVIRONMENT

Have shelves within easy reach of the children for keeping the materials. The preparation of the environment for the world of physics is relatively simple once you have gathered all of the apparatus necessary for the various experiments.

At any one time you will have only three or four of the physical experiments or sensorial keys on the physics shelves. Present them as beautifully as you would any other work. Change them when they are no longer being used.

There should be plastic mats for working with the water experiments. Keep an extra supply of small objects for the sink and float and magnet exercise. Keep these somewhere other than in the classroom and change the objects often to keep the experiments more interesting.

Pictures for the Walls

Have beautiful pictures having to do with scientists and inventors and inventions hanging on the walls at the eye level of the child. Change them often.

Books

Have books connected with physics principles such as sound, magnetism or sink and float, rivers, oceans, rocks, etc., and books about inventions and scientists and inventors. There should be simple picture books and books with more text for the older readers in the class.

Rather than keeping the language materials or books near these experiments, because of possible damage connected with the water exercises, have a section in your book corner with science books having to do with physics, and the classified language material.

CARING FOR THE PHYSICS AREA

Some of the most important lessons in any Montessori primary class have to do with taking care of oneself (dressing, cleaning nose, etc.), taking care of the environment (handing materials carefully, sweeping, etc.), and taking care of others by being considerate, kind, and polite. In each of the culture areas the teacher develops and teaches the children specific activities having to do with that area of the room. These are called the practical life lessons.

Following are some ideas of practical life exercises that can be provided that relate to taking care of the physics area of the classroom. Before showing the child a physics activity, be sure that you practice it yourself, perhaps giving the lesson to another adult, so that it will be logical, clear, and possible, for the child.

Drying the objects in the sink and float activity

Drying the material, the table, etc., for all of the water activities

Carrying material

Opening and closing boxes

Pouring water

Polishing the magnifying glass

Washing hands

Dusting shelves

Dusting material

Putting material back on the shelves properly

Polishing material

Sweeping

Rolling up the "walkie-talkie"

A PERSONAL EXAMPLE

In designing any practical life activity for the child you must first think about the stage of development and the age of the child you are planning for. Then think about all of the elements of the lesson, such as the material, the steps of the presentation, the control of error (so the child can independently see if it has been done correctly), the points of consciousness (sometimes called pedagogical notes) that are steps that you discover, as you practice, need special attention ahead of, or during, a lesson. Then gather the material and practice the activity yourself.

When you analyze the steps of the lesson you may want to include as many as possible so you know what skills the child needs to have mastered before he is ready for this lesson.

The following is a briefly analyzed lesson:

Opening and Closing a Box

Material: A small box with a fitted lid — perhaps the box of objects for the magnet activity

Presentation:

(The box is on the table in front of the child and you)

1. Show the child your left hand as you move it toward the box.

2. Grasp the box firmly toward the bottom, with your thumb on one side and your other fingers on the opposite side.

3. Show the child your right hand.

4. Move your right hand toward the box.

5. Grasp the lid firmly with your thumb on one side and your other fingers on the opposite side of the lid.

6. Holding the box with your left hand, lift the lid straight up, slowly.

7. Stop about 5 inches above the box; pause, and move the lid back down slowly.

8. As you move the lid toward the box, show that it is exactly above the box, and that the corners of the lid and box are opposite one another if it is a square or rectangular box.

9. Fit the lid gently on the box.

10. Let go of the lid and the box.

Control of Error: Getting the lid on the box correctly

Points of Consciousness:

1. The lid must not fit too tightly on the box.

2. The child must grasp the box firmly as he lifts the lid.

3. The lid must be put back on slowly and loosely and not be forced.

4. Do not talk during the lesson.

This last point is of course true of any lesson given at this age. The child can only focus completely on watching or listening. If, during a lesson, it is necessary to say something or the child says something, then stop moving your hands and wait till the speaking is finished.

A good way to see if you have analyzed and described the steps correctly is to ask a friend to pretend to be a child. Then have her do exactly as you say as you read the steps.

Purpose: To aid muscular development in making light movements, eye-hand coordination, and concentration

Age: The sensorial keys or experiments can be taught at various ages. Be sure to adapt each to the ability of the child

SENSORIAL KEYS
THE PHYSICS EXPERIMENTS

A sensorial key is something that unlocks a door to a piece of the world that can be directly experienced through the senses of sight, touch, smell, sound, or taste, rather than through the imagination. They build the foundation for later abstract thinking about the world. The physics experiments are the sensorial keys for the world of physics; and should be simple activities, related to the child's needs, fitted to his age, and easy enough that he can do them himself. They should feed his curiosity and bring forth the fact that there are certain natural laws which are unchanging, at least unchanging at this level. The keys should be simple, limited, and isolating one point to be made clear.

Do not bring in complicated experiments, science kits, etc., at this stage. All of the necessary equipment should be such that it could be found in the home. The keys should lead the child to find out for himself, which he does by repeating the experiments.

The experiments are kept in the same kind of organization as any of the other material in the Montessori classroom, on lovely trays and containers made of wood or glass or metal, avoiding plastic whenever possible. Have perhaps three or four experiments on the shelves at a time, changing them when you notice that the children are no longer using them.

What age? First of all consider the safety of the child. The age when specific experiments are given depends on the experiment, the level of development of the child, and his interests. Remember that these experiments must not become "water" play or other play, but they should be respected as important work just as is all of the other work in the Montessori environment. The purpose must be clear so the child can work toward a goal. He must be old enough to carry out each experiment with the purpose for which it is intended so he will grasp the concept and the physics principle that the experiment reveals.

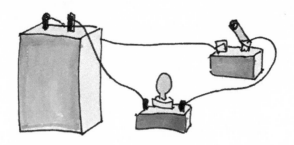

Simple Circuit

Materials:

A 4.5 – 6 volt battery with two poles covered with caps that can be screwed on and off

A switch mounted on a wooden block

A small light mounted on a wooden block

Three insulated wires about 8 inches long (These wear out with use. You will need more)

Aim:

To show that the circuit must be complete to work and that if it is broken the light will not turn on.

Before the Presentation:

Explain to the child that he should not experiment with batteries and switches in the home. Explain that this one is absolutely safe but appliances at home are not.

Presentation for a very young child:

Have the circuit assembled and just show that the switch turns the light on and off.

Presentation for an older Child:

1: Have the circuit assembled and disconnect one of the terminals on the battery and turn the switch on and off. Nothing happens. Disconnect the other terminal. Same thing.

2: Take the light bulb out of the socket and turn the switch on and off. Nothing happens. Put the light bulb back and try the switch. The light turns on.

3 for the oldest child: The child can take the circuit completely apart with a screwdriver and put it back together.

4 for the oldest child: Hold various objects — an eraser, a paper clip, etc. — between a pole on the battery and the wire. See which objects complete the circuit.

Language:

Give the names of the parts of the circuit. Do not give explanations. If the child asks why this works, say something like, "I don't know. Isn't it amazing!" (We are not physicists.)

Points of Consciousness:

Make sure that the circuit is kept disconnected while in the box.

Before giving the lesson be sure that the switch is in the "off" position.

Shadows

Materials:

The Simple Circuit

A white piece of cardboard about one foot square secured in a wooden stand or mounted in such a way that it is vertical.

Aim: A natural introduction to shadows

Presentation:

Place the Simple Circuit on the table.

Place the electric circuit a few feet away.

Hold your hand or various objects between the circuit light and the white cardboard to produce shadows.

Next hold the object steady between the light and the cardboard and move the light around to see how the shadow changes on the cardboard.

Magnet Sorting

Materials:

A small, strong magnet

The "key", which is the little piece of metal that goes across the ends of the magnet

A box of objects, i.e. paper clips, chalk, hair pins, buttons, tin, plastic, another magnet, etc., about half of the objects that will be attracted to the magnet and half that will not be attracted.

Aim:

To give a natural introduction to magnetism.

Presentation:

Spread the objects on the table, preferably on a felt "table mat".

Take the key off of the magnet and place it back in the box.

Very slowly, as if you do not know what the results will be, move the magnet down toward one of the objects

If this objects sticks, move it to one side of the table mat.

Repeat with each of the objects, placing the objects that are attracted to the magnet to one side of the table mat and those that are not attracted to the other side.

Exercise 1: Some of the objects in the first presentation can become magnetized.

Make a chain of paper clips, the first one attached to the magnet, and then the others in a chain of magnetized paper clips. Try this with the other objects to see if others will become magnetized.

Exercise 2: Explore the room with the magnet to see which surfaces and objects attract the magnet.

Exercise 3: You will need a piece of cardboard about 1 foot square.

Control a paper clip or other object through a piece of cardboard. Place the small metallic object on top of the cardboard. Hold the magnet against the cardboard on the underneath side so that the metal object is attracted to the magnet. Move the magnet around against the cardboard and the child will see the object on top moving.

Point of Consciousness: If the key is not kept on the magnet the magnet becomes weaker.

Sand and Iron Filings

Materials:

A magnet

A small jar containing a small amount of iron filings

A small jar containing a small amount of white or light-colored sand

A plate or saucer

A handkerchief or piece of thin white fabric about 5″ square

Presentation:

Pour the sand and iron filings from the jars onto the plate

Wrap the magnet in the cloth

Move the magnet slowly over all of the sand until all of the iron filings have been picked up.

Still holding firmly on the magnet and cloth place them in the iron filings jar so when you remove the magnet from the cloth all of the filings will fall into the jar.

Remove the magnet from the cloth

Point of Consciousness:

Be sure to keep the magnet wrapped in the cloth, as it is very difficult to remove iron filings from a magnet.

The jars should be wide enough that the magnet in cloth will fit inside to remove the filings.

Keep extra sand and iron filings in a storage area outside of the classroom

Compass

Materials:

A needle and a piece of cork to hold the needle while in the box or on the tray

A magnet

A large clear glass bowl of water

A small piece of paper with an arrow pointing to the letter "N" on one of the edges

A plastic lid or something else that will float and hold the paper and needle

Aim: Natural introduction to the compass

Presentation:

Magnetize the needle by moving it in ONE direction only along ONE pole of the magnet.

Draw the compass face, the "N" for north, on the piece of paper

Place the paper on the lid

Either place the needle on the north-south line on the paper, or if the paper is thin enough stick the needle through the paper to secure it in this position

Float the lid-paper-needle on the surface of the water

Wait as the needle finds the direction

Show the child how to empty the bowl of water, and dry everything before putting away.

Control of Error:

Have a small compass to see if the needle is pointing in the correct direction

Further Activity:

Sometimes cardboard puzzle maps in the home have "north" marked. In this case you can show the child, with either the homemade compass or a real one, how to position a puzzle so that "N" on the puzzle is facing real north. Some teachers also mark the Montessori puzzle maps in the classroom with an "N" and show the child how to do this.

Points of Consciousness:

Definitely practice ahead of time

Sometimes the lid-paper-needle gets stuck against the edge of the bowl of water and needs to be nudged back to floating freely on the surface of the water

A plastic mat and cloth for drying is kept on the physics shelves for all water experiments

Making a compass is something hikers learn to do if they get lost, using a magnet and needle and a leaf to float on water. There are YouTube videos about this.

Age: This is for an older child who has experience with a needle and can create the compass on his own sometime after the presentation

Empty Bottle

Materials:

Plastic table mat and drying cloth

Large clear glass bowl of water

An empty bottle

Aim: To show that the bottle is not really empty and that the air has to come out before the water can go in.

Presentation:

Show the child the bottle.

Ask what is in it, as you show clearly that it is "empty"

Slowly lower the bottle into the water in a vertical position with the mouth of the bottle down

Then slowly tilt is so that the air begins to escape

Watch the bubbles of air rise to the surface as the bottle slowly fills with water.

Show the child how to empty the bowl of water and dry everything before putting away.

Point of Consciousness:

Be sure that the bottle is the correct size to clearly show the bubbles rising to the top of the water

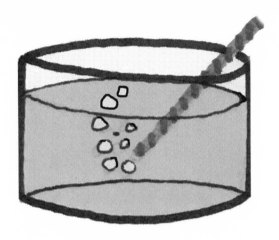

Blowing Bubbles

Materials:

The large glass bowl with water

A plastic mat and drying cloth

A box of paper drinking straws (not plastic)

Presentation:

Stick the end of a straw far into the bowl of water.

Blow through it slowly, making bubbles rise to the surface of the water.

When you are finished show the child how to break the straw in half and throw it in a wastebasket.

Tell the child he can select a straw and use it as long as he likes, breaking it in half and throwing it away when he is finished.

Everything is dried and put away when finished.

Blowing A Boat

Materials:

The large glass bowl with water

A plastic mat and drying cloth

A walnut shell half

A toothpick

A small piece of plasticine

A small triangle of paper for making a sail

A paper straw

Presentation:

Show the child how to make the little boat: stick the toothpick through the triangle of paper and then secure it in the piece of plasticine in the walnut shell.

Place the boat on the surface of the water.

Blow air through the straw onto the sail in order to move the boat over the water.

Do this from several directions, different angles.

The child can leave the boat in a small plate for the next child.

Dry everything and put it away when finished.

Candle in Limited Air

Materials:

A plate or saucer deep enough to hold 1/3 cup of water

A piece of candle secured to the middle of the saucer

A small pitcher of colored water (colored with food coloring or paint)

A small glass that fits over the candle with an inch or so over the flame to spare.

A box of matches

Presentation:

Pour a little of the colored water into the saucer at the base of the candle.

Light the candle and watch it glow

Place the glass quickly on the saucer, upside down covering the candle, the edge of the glass in the colored water.

Watch the water rise inside the glass and the candle go out.

Points of Consciousness:

It is a good idea, until some of the older children have learned to use matches safely, that the directress do this experiment, but as often as the children want to see it. So keep the material out of the classroom.

Note:

I have often done this at special family meals and it is always enjoyed. It was here that I learned my lesson about answering a child's question. I had always thought that the reason the candle goes out is because the fire uses up the oxygen. But one year my physicist son-in-law told us, at the family meal, that that is not the reason. It took me to Google to research. The reason the candle goes out is very complicated. Once again this is why the pat answer to a child's answer about why something happens during a physics experiment is, "I don't know, but isn't it interesting?"

Bicycle Pump

Materials:

A manual bicycle pump

Presentation:

Experiment with showing how the air is forced through the tube by exerting pressure on the handle.

Show what happens when you place a finger over the nozzle where the air comes out.

Make bubbles with it by placing the end under water.

Use it to inflate a bicycle tire.

Aim:

This is a natural introduction to the movement of air. This is one of these common household items that we take for granted but that are a valuable physics activity.

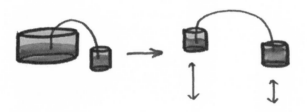

Syphoning

Materials:

Plastic tablemat and drying cloth

A bowl of colored water

Two glass jars

A short, approximately 12" length of very soft, pliable rubber tubing

Presentation:

Put the tube in the large bowl of water. This must be done very carefully, placing the middle of the tube down first, so the tube fills completely with water and there are no air pockets.

Pinch one of the ends of the tube under water.

Lift it out, letting no water out or air in.

Place the end in the jar that is held lower than the bowl of water.

Pinch the other end under water and put it in the other jar.

Then move the two jars alternately up and down and the water will flow back and forth from one jar to the other. You can see the water levels rise and fall.

Dry everything completely when finished.

Points of Consciousness:

The tubing must be soft enough so that even a child can easily pinch the end together preventing any water from escaping as the pinched end of the tube is placed in the small jar.

Be sure that you practice this and can do it easily before showing a child

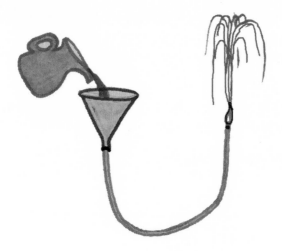

Funnel

Materials:

Plastic tablemat and drying cloth

A basin such as that used for washing cloths, etc.

A small pitcher of water

A length of rubber tubing

A small funnel hooked (or taped if the fit is not perfect) to one end of rubber tubing

The other end of the tube is fastened (or taped) to the glass part of an eyedropper.

Presentation:

Have the child hold the end of the tube with the eyedropper attached over the basin

Hold the funnel at the same height and slowly pour water from the pitcher into the funnel

As you slowly pour the water raise and lower the funnel to see how the water pressure in the "fountain" of water coming out of the eye dropper changes as you raise and lower the funnel.

Refill the pitcher and repeat, inviting the child to do the pouring as you hold the funnel and tube.

Dry everything and put it away.

Vacuum

Materials:

Plastic tablemat and drying cloth

A small glass jar

A pitcher of water holding a little more water than will fit in the jar

A piece of cardboard a little larger than the mouth of the jar

A Basin

Presentation:

Pour the water from the pitcher into the jar, very slowly toward the end of the pouring so it is clear that it is absolutely full. Add the water a tiny bit at a time at the end to make the point that the surface of the water is slightly concave (above the top of the jar).

Place the piece of cardboard over the top of the jar.

Lift the jar holding the cardboard in place.

Turn it over, still holding the cardboard in place, everything held over the basin.

Remove your hand. The cardboard will stick to the jar keeping the water from pouring out.

Exercise 1:

Do everything the same except when you turn the jar over do it quickly and do not hold the cardboard in place with your hand. The cardboard will still stick if you do it correctly.

cut →

Rising Hot Air

Materials:

A round piece of paper 3-5 inches in diameter

Scissors

A stick that is long enough for the spiral to hang down completely with room to spare, maybe 18 inches

A heater of some sort, such as a floor heating vent or space heater

Presentation:

Cut a spiral out of the round piece of paper

Fasten the center of the spiral to the end of the stick. The end can just be balanced on the end of the stick or it can be fastened with a pin

Fasten the other end of the stick to a piece of wood or something to make it stand up. This can be done in either case with a piece of plasticine

Place the stick and spiral on the heat source and watch the spiral turn as the heat passes through it.

Points of Consciousness:

The circle does not have to be perfect. It can be roughly drawn by you and later by a child.

The cutting is the same. It is more important for a child to see that he can make this himself than for it to be perfect.

Experiment with all stages before showing a child.

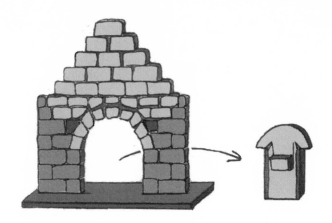

The Arch

Materials:

This is a piece of Montessori didactic material, found from AMI approved Montessori materials manufacturers and found in most schools. It consists of a base on which about half of the arch is constructed, a number of small wooden blocks to build the arch, and a movable "guide" that the arch is built on top of.

Presentation:

This work is usually done on a felt tablemat.

Position the "guide" in the middle of the base.

Lay out all of the pieces, sorting them on to matching blocks

Build the arch over the guide.

Press your hand down on the top of the blocks to show how sturdy the arch is.

Remove the guide.

Again press your hand down on the top of the blocks to show that the shape of the blocks makes the arch sturdy.

Language:

You can tell an older child that the special "keystone" is the block that supports the arch.

Camera

Materials:

A magnifying glass

Presentation: Show the child how to explore the details of the room with the magnifying glass

Exercise 1: Do the same with the lens of a camera or old glasses lenses

Exercise 2: A pinhole camera can also be made. The directions for a simple one can be found in a science book or on the Internet

Aim: a simple introduction to the bending of light in glass

Sound

Materials:

A long piece of garden hose, perhaps 6-10 feet

Presentation:

Use this as a speaking tube to transmit your voice as you whisper into one end and the other end is held to the ear of a child.

Show the child how to listen to other sounds through it, such as the ticking of a clock or the dripping of water from a faucet.

Exercise 1: Ear on the table. Show the child how much more easily sound is transmitted through wood by having him put one ear on the end of a large table as you tap with your finger or a pencil on the other end.

Exercise 2: Making a "Walkie-Talkie"

To prepare these materials ahead of time or with the children if you decide to do this: with a nail and hammer, punch a hole in the end of each of two empty, clean, and safe food cans. Eight-ounce cans work well.

Tie knots and thread the ends of 5-8 feet of waxed or other slightly insulated string or cord between two cans.

Talk into one end while the other end is held to a child's ear.

You will notice that, unlike with the piece of garden hose, the string usually needs to be stretched taut in order for this to work.

Show the child how to wind the cord around one of the cans when putting it away

Sink and Float

Materials:

Plastic tablemat

A large bowl

Pitcher for water

A cloth for drying objects

A box of objects such as a piece of wood, a piece of chalk, a coin, piece of plasticine, a screw, etc. Have several objects that will sink and several that will float.

Have extras of each so each time a child does the activity he will make a discovery.

Presentation:

Place the bowl and the cloth on the tablemat

Fill the bowl with water

Place the box of objects between you and the bowl

One by one remove the objects from the box and drop in the bowl to see if they sink or float.

As you remove each object carefully dry it.

Place the objects that float on one side of the tablemat, and those that sink on the other side.

Be sure to do this with as much interest as if it is the first time you are making these discoveries.

Exercise 1:

One day as you are doing this work, drop the piece of plasticine into the water. It will sink. Then remove it and shape it into a little bowl or boat and gently place it on the surface of the water. This time it will float.

Be sure that you do not give a long involved explanation; just let the child make the discovery.

Pendulum

Materials:

A long piece of string, maybe 2-3 feet in length

A weight of some kind tied to the end of the string. A "plumb bob" or "plummet, used by builders as a vertical preference line or plumb-line works well.

Presentation:

Hold the string and slowly begin to make the weight sway back and forth.

Have one person clap as the weight reaches each extreme in the swinging arc.

Hold the string at different distances from the weight, again someone clapping as it reaches each extreme in the arc.

The claps will be closer together as the string is held closer to the weight.

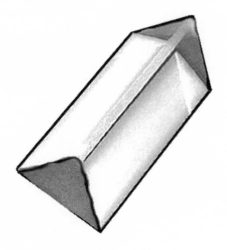

Prism

Materials:

A 2-3 inch glass prism

Presentation:

On a sunny day put a triangular glass prism next to the window in such a way that the children can see the color spectrum on a wall. Just set it up and let the children discover it.

LANGUAGE

(See the Language chapter for details and illustrations)

Spoken Language and Vocabulary

There is specific language for all of the areas of the classrooms. For the world of physics give the children very simple but accurate language to go with all of the experiments, including the exact names of the pieces of equipment.

"Why does this happen?" It is very important to avoid giving simplified brief explanations when asked why something happens in the carrying out of an experiment. The experiments are to be experienced by the children but not explained by the adult. Discoveries in the world of all sciences are continuing today and simple explanations can halt the child's curiosity to know more about how matter acts and why. When a child asks, "Why" (does sound travel through the top of a table for example) you might say, "I don't know. Isn't it interesting?" We want to inspire a sense of wonder and the desire to explore and to learn more.

Pre-reading Classified Pictures

This material helps increase the child's vocabulary and helps with classification of objects in his world. Here are some examples in the area of physics:

A set with pictures of the materials, bowl, cloth, magnet, or objects used in sink and float, etc.

Sets of pictures of inventions such as kinds of cars, boats, other vehicles. Pictures of scientists and inventors.

Classified Pictures Reading Stage or 3-Part Cards

The same pictures used at the pre-reading stage are now used to create the first physics reading cards. You will see in the language chapter that this allows a child to check and correct his own work, repeating it as he likes to make the learning secure.

Pictures Showing "Parts of" with 3-Part Cards

This is another set of 3-part cards, with one part on each card, such "battery", "switch", light bulb", "wire" for the electric circuit.

Pictures Showing "Parts of" with a Large Picture of the Whole Object

This is another way of showing, thinking about, labeling, and the parts of an object. On a large piece of card the whole picture is shown and the child places the labels, checking his work when he is finished by comparing his work with an identical large piece of card with the parts labeled.

Again an example could be the parts of the electric circuit or one of the other physics experiments. If there is an invention common to the culture of your children, such as a bicycle is in Holland, you could create either a reading chart such as with the electric circuit above, or you could create 2-part cards that show the main parts of the bicycle. This is easier to do with the large card method that shows the entire object or bicycle. Other examples include the parts of the Roman Arch, or the bicycle pump experiment materials.

Definition Reading Stages

You could create definitions of these parts of the bicycle or whatever is familiar to the children

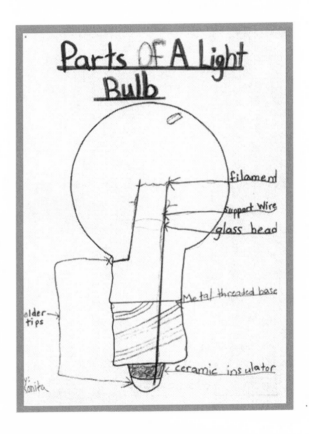

FURTHER ACTIVITIES
IN THE WORLD OF PHYSICS

Children may want to make their own materials after doing an experiment, such as little boats with sails, paper circle for heat rising, a compass, or they might want to bring in other items to try with the sink and float or magnet attraction.

For written work the child who is not yet writing can follow up the experiments with drawings. In the above picture a child, interested in the electric circuit, has learned the names of all of the parts of a light bulb and drawn and labeled this part of the experiment.

For a child who is interested in writing he could carry out the experiment and then draw it. Or list the materials, or even combine a drawing, and the steps made to carry out the experiment.

Although "going out" or field trips is more appropriate at the 6-12 level, it might be possible to take the children on very special visits linking these keys to the environment, such as to a museum to see a Foucault Pendulum.

THE WORLD OF BOTANY

*N*o description, no image in any book can replace the sight of real trees and all the life to be found around them in a real forest. Something emanates from those trees which speaks to the soul, something no book, no museum, can give. The forest reveals that it is not only the trees that exist, but a whole, inter-related collection of lives.

—Montessori, *Childhood to Adolescence*

Botany is the study of plants. The purposes for giving this experience to young children are many. Being in touch with nature is healthy for a child in many ways and observation of plants teaches important life lessons to human beings at any age. Specifically this work is meant to help children become familiar with different types of plants and to learn how to care for plants. Through this work and gardening and growing food, children come to realize that plants are necessary for our survival. This is indirect preparation of this study for the future, to foster an interest in not destroying the plant world as humans expand over the earth.

PREPARING THE ENVIRONMENT

We must adapt to the local conditions, but ideally there should be a nice, light, airy classroom that opens out onto a lovely garden, and the world of plants is one area where we consider both the outside and inside environment.

The Outside Environment

Wild Area

Have an area as wild as possible. Plant wild flowers and grasses, specimens from different families and groups. Some of the best nature specimens are plants that cannot be cultivated, that we call weeds. Trees are good for climbing but first climb them yourself to make sure they are safe. If they are too tall to be safe, cut some of the branches off at the safe point so children can go no further. Don't have a pond because you want children to be able to go out into the garden on their own without supervision.

Cultivated Area

The cultivated part of the garden should consist of lawn (if recommended in your area), paths wide enough for tricycles to pass, and a garden ideally with a path along both sides. Have plants that correspond with the in-class materials (like leaf classification or parts of the flower). Have as many varieties of plants as you can to make this area rich for discovery. Provide each child with their own patch of earth for flowers, vegetables, and fruit. Be sure that this patch is small enough that the child can reach everything without having to step on it. Encourage the children to grow things to eat or use.

Have a little tool shed or cupboard to keep tools in an orderly way. Provide real tools cut to the child's size, such as a real adult hoe with the handle cut to his size. Have materials for cleaning and caring for the tools. Have baskets for gathering things. Have a wheelbarrow for moving things, making sure that paths in the garden are wide enough for a wheelbarrow. Have a water source that the children can use independently. Provide a boot scraper near the door

The Inside Environment

The environment for the child from age 2.5-6 is called the "children's house", the English translation of the Italian "casa dei bambini." It should have the look and feel of a house rather than a classroom. Plants, arranged just as they would be in a home, in pots on the floor or cabinets, or hanging from the ceiling, contribute to this feeling.

Be sure and research the safety of plants in your part of the world before bringing them into the environment. Also take into consideration the variety that will introduce the child to leaf shapes, etc., that he will be learning about.

Have a place in the classroom for everything connected with the world of plants, including materials for caring for the plants and experiments that address the needs and functions of plants.

Have a Nature Table, for use with only one theme at a time, such as fall leaves or a botany experiment. Try to change this often, once a week or more often, so it remains interesting. Children should be encouraged to bring in plants and other specimens for the nature table. If you do not have an accessible outside area expand the nature table.

Provide a place on the botany shelf for experiment data (the drawings and recording the progress of an experiment)

Have a variety of plants in the classroom, of course researching safety of the plants. A little sign "I have been watered" to place next to the stem of a potted plant keeps it from being drowned.

Collect a variety of vases, shallow bowls, flowerpots, tools, watering cans, etc.

Consider the seasons and be seasonal in providing flowers, fruit, vegetables – growing and using – to help the child experience the passage of time and the changes during a year.

Have shelves for the pre-reading botany picture collections, classified reading cards.

Pictures for the Walls

Have beautiful pictures of flowers, herbs, and trees. These can be photographs, reproductions of paintings, or images from great art masterpieces, both realistic and abstract. They should be hung at the eye level of the child and changed often.

Books

Have books connected with the world of plants. Keep language materials and books connected with botany in this area, sometimes placing a book or two in the book corner. There should be simple picture books and books with more text for the older readers in the class.

Here are some suggestions for books in this area:

Stories about herbs

Stories about gardens

A book about gardening

A book about plants that feed us

Plants that grow in different climactic zones such as the rain forest, cold lands, deserts, and mountains

Books about one subject, such as trees, grasses, garden flowers, cacti, wild flowers, ferns

A children's picture encyclopedia can be found that has clear and interesting pictures of some of the subjects we cover, such as parts of the leaf, parts of the flower, and so on. These are usually intended for the older child and adult but they can definitely have a place in the Montessori primary class.

CARING FOR THE BOTANY AREA

Following are some ideas of practical life exercises that can be provided that relate to taking care of the botany area of the classroom. Before showing the child an activity, be sure that you practice it yourself, perhaps giving the lesson to another adult, so that it will be logical, clear, possible, for the child.

OUTSIDE ENVIRONMENT

Raking leaves

Cutting dead leaves from plants

Cutting dead flowers from plants "deadheading"

Watering plants

Straightening up garden tools

Cleaning, oiling, caring for garden tools

INSIDE ENVIRONMENT

Watering plants

Cutting and arranging flowers

Changing the water in flower arrangements

Dusting the leaves of plants

Dusting the nature table

Dusting and polishing the leaf cabinet

Dusting and straightening up the bookshelf

Removing dead leaves from plants

A PERSONAL EXAMPLE

In designing any practical life activity for the child you must first analyze the stages of the development of the age of the child you are planning for. Think about all of the elements of any practical life lesson, such as the material, the steps of the presentation, the control of error (so the child can independently see if it has been done correctly), the points of consciousness (sometimes called pedagogical notes. These are points that you discover need special attention ahead of or during a lesson), the purpose, and the age. Then gather the material and practice the activity yourself.

When you analyze the steps of the lesson you may want to include as many as possible until you know what skills the child needs to have mastered before he is ready for this lesson. The following is a briefly analyzed lesson.

Removing Dead Leaves from a Plant

Material: a potted plant with a few dead leaves that have fallen. A wastebasket.

Presentation:

(The wastebasket is placed on the floor near the plant. The child can do this wherever a plant is kept if it is within easy reach.)

1. Show the child the thumb and first finger of your right hand, with which you are going to pick up the dead leaves.

2. Place your whole left hand against the left side of the pot to steady it.

3. Point to a dead leaf, make a sad face

4. Carefully and slowly pick up the leaf.

5. Move the hand with the leaf to just above the wastebasket.

6. Let go of the leaf so it falls into the wastebasket.

7. Move your hand back to near the plant.

8. Repeat steps 3-7 with other leaves that have fallen, or invite the child to pick up these.

9. With the child look for another plant so he can do the work.

Control of Error:

Getting all of the dead leaves from under the plant into the wastebasket. Visual check.

Points of Consciousness:

1. Be sure there are at least one, preferably, two plants that need this attention.

2. The child must be able to distinguish between dead and live leaves.

3. He must have enough control of movement not to knock over the plant.

4. Be sure the child understands where to put the leaves.

Purpose: To aid development of the control of movement, eye-hand coordination, and concentration

Age: 2.5 years onward

SENSORIAL KEYS: NATURE TABLE, BOTANY EXPERIMENTS, AND THE LEAF CABINET

THE NATURE TABLE

This part of the botany area is very important. When I was taking my training in London many years ago and spending some days observing in a very good class, the nature table for that week contained 3 to 4 four drawings, by children, of birds. It was clear that they had "copied" the drawings, freehand, from a bird book that lay on the table with the drawings. They were colored in with colored pencils and quite beautiful. This introduced me not only to the idea of something that could be placed on a nature table, but to the artistic potential of young children when they are not given coloring books, printed outlines made by adults, or any other kind of an adult-produced model to copy.

The nature table should be a source of inspiration for all that goes on in the nature corner of the environment. It should be a small table of a height so that even the youngest child can observe what is on it. Generally there should be just one item or items in just one category on the nature table at a time. The table should be changed daily or weekly and children encouraged to bring in their own plants for a visit on the nature table. If you have an outside garden there will be changing projects there but if there is no outside garden then you will enlarge your nature table and have more on it at any one time. Of course it should be kept beautiful and clean.

BOTANY EXPERIMENTS

Here is a list of botany experiments appropriate for introducing the world of plants. These may be kept on the nature table or on a window shelf, depending on what else is on the nature table at any one time, or the need of a particular experiment. These are chosen carefully and have been tested for many years, each experiment bringing one aspect of botany to the child's attention. Always give the most precise language possible connected with the nature table, the experiments, and classified pictures. For example give the names of the seeds and beans used in the experiments, not just "little seeds" or "beans."

These are sensorial experiences, to experience during this stage of development, not to understand. Do not give simplified explanations for what occurs. These experiments lay the sensorial foundation for intelligent questions followed by more complicated experiments, scientific research, and discoveries; this is the work that will be done in the elementary class.

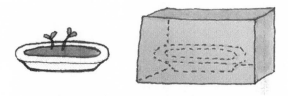

Experiment 1 – Needs of the Plant, no Light

Plant mustard seeds (or some other fast growing seed) in two saucers or small, wide jars with soil. Give one light, warmth, and water. Deprive the second container of seeds of light by putting a box over it. Continue to give both warmth and water. Compare the two as they grow, and show the children how to carefully lift the box to see what is happening when there is no light.

Experiment 2 – Needs of the Plant, no Water

Plant mustard seeds in two saucers or small, wide jars with soil. Give the first light, warmth, and water. Deprive the second one of water, giving it the same warmth and light as the first. Compare the two as they grow (or do not grow).

Experiment 3 – Needs of the Plant, no Warmth

Plant mustard seeds in two saucers or small, wide jars with soil. Give one light, warmth, and water. Deprive the second of warmth by putting it outside on a window ledge but within view if in a cold season so it will have light. Compare the growth after a time. If there is no cold season you could get one saucer where the seeds are not to be given warmth out during the morning and then let the children see you put it in the refrigerator for the afternoon and overnight.

Experiment 4 – Needs of the Plant, no Soil

Plant mustard seeds in a deep saucer filled with soil. Put the same number and kind of seeds in another deep saucer with no soil, just on a piece of white paper or cotton. Give both saucers water, warmth, and light. Compare the growth after awhile.

Experiment 5 – Gravitropism, Roots Grow Downward

Collect three small glass jars. Prepare them in such a way that you will be able to place a seed in each that will be held against the glass. You can do this by filling the jars with cotton balls, or else a rolled up piece of paper with sand in the middle pressing the paper against the glass. In each jar place one large bean. One right side up, one upside down, one sidewise. Give all warmth, light, and water. If you are not sure that the beans are going to sprout you can soak them in water overnight to see the root begin to swell. Or if you need to soak them for two nights be sure to change the water and keep it fresh for the second night.

Note what happens to the roots, the cotyledons, as they begin to grow. The term for roots growing downward, *gravitropism*, Latin "gravis" for "heavy" and "tropus" for "a turning", can be given to the child but do not explain "why" this happens. That is for much later.

Experiment 6 – Phototropism
– Leaves Grow toward the Light

Plant quick growing seed such as cress in 1-3 small jars or plant pots. Place them in a cardboard box with a lid so they will receive no light but give them warmth and water. When the plants are an inch or two tall cut a little window near one end of the lid and replace it on top of the box. Keep the plants watered for a few days and you will see the plants grow toward the hole in the lid, toward the light. You can give the name *phototropism* Greek "photo" for light, and "tropus" for a turning, but do not explain "why" leaves grow toward the light. That is for much later.

Experiment 7 – Negative Phototropism
– Roots Grow away from Light

Plant mustard seeds in two jam jars. Cover one jar with black paper wrapped around the jar so no light can get to the side of the jar. Give both jars warmth and water and light. In the uncovered jar the roots will grow straight down. In the covered jar see which way the roots grow. Aside from growing down toward the earth roots also grow away from light.

Experiment 8 – Growing a Plant from Part of a Root

Cut off the tops of carrots, parsnips, sweet potato, that have begun to sprout greenery. Stick 4 toothpicks around the middle of the piece you have cut off so it can be held on top of a glass or glass jar. Fill the jar with water so that the bottom of the piece of root is always under water. The water must be changed regularly. This can make a lovely plant and when it stops growing can sometimes be successfully transferred to a pot of soil to continue growing.

Note: We do not give a seed lesson with one seed in each paper cup for each child — an experiment that I remember from childhood. When this is done, through no fault of a child, some seeds will germinate and some will not, and some will be under-watered and some overwatered. This can be sad for the children. Each of the above experiments belongs to the whole group and is taken care of collectively.

THE LEAF CABINET

The leaf cabinet is a standard piece of material for any Montessori primary class. Its construction has been overseen for many years and it is available from approved Montessori materials makers. Its use is part of AMI Montessori teacher training but here is an example of how it is used in the classroom.

Material: A wooden cabinet 10 centimeters tall, 31 centimeters wide and 40 centimeters long. The cabinet has six drawers, each containing several wooden insets and frames of the shapes of leaves.

List of leaves in the cabinet: ovate, obovate, cordate, obcordate, triangulate, orbiculate, elliptical, lanceolate, reniform, hastate, aciculate, spatulate, and linear

Aims: To give a key for classifying experiences and an incentive to go out and explore. Visual discrimination, the eye getting practice in recognizing shapes. Preparation of the hand for writing, especially the wrist as the shapes of the inset and frame are felt with two fingers.

Presentation 1: Show the child how to take a drawer carefully out of the leaf cabinet and replace it, slowly with both hands. Let him do it.

Place a drawer on a table, partly on a tablemat. Take out one of the leaf insets holding the knob by your left hand. Show the child the first two fingers of your right hand. With these fingers feel around the edge of the inset very slowly starting at the edge nearest you. Then feel around the frame of that particular inset in the same slow way, using two fingers and your wrist turning to enable the fingers to make their careful progress. Replace the leaf inset and go on with the other leaf shapes in the drawer.

Presentation 2: Take out all of the leaf insets in one drawer and place them on the mat in front of you. One by one feel an inset and frame and then place the leaf inset in the corresponding frame. Depending on the child this might be enough or you can suggest that he put this drawer back and do another drawer. He can do each of the 6 drawers one at a time.

Presentation 3: After he can do each drawer separately suggest that he do 2 at once, then 3, until he can place all 6 drawers on 2 floor mats, remove all of the leaf insets, mix them up, and replace them. He should continue to feel the leaf inset and the corresponding frame each time.

Presentation 4: Start again with one drawer at a time, but this time show the child how to use a blindfold and replace the leaf insets blindfolded.

Language: The names of the leaf shapes in the leaf cabinet can be taught by three period lessons as soon as the child is starting to work with the leaf cabinet cards. They should have heard these names in connection with real leaves first.

Further Activities: When the child is at the stage where he is beginning to work with the cards and is learning the names of the leaf shapes, two activities that come at about the same time. Then collect real leaves and classify them if you have not done this before.

First classify leaves according to the shapes learned with the leaf cabinet then go on to classify them according to margins, attachments, etc.

It is very important that you only work with one classification at a time.

Cards for the Leaf Cabinet

There are also three sets of cards the size of the individual frames that hold the leaf insets.

Set 1: solid colored inset figures

Set 2: thickly outlined inset figures

Set 3: thin outlines of the inset figures

Note: Just as the learning about the Geometric Cabinet and cards is part of the Sensorial Album part of the AMI Montessori teacher-training course, so are the Leaf Cabinet and Cards. There is a grand scheme of when each piece of sensorial material is presented based on careful observation of each child, what he has learned before this lesson, parallel activities in other areas of the classroom, and so on. So beyond the brief explanation of the Leaf Cabinet given above, it would be better to learn about the cards in a full diploma course.

(See the Language chapter for details and illustrations)

LANGUAGE

(See the Language chapter for details and illustrations)

Spoken Language and Vocabulary

There is specific language for all of the areas of the classrooms. For the world of physics give the children very simple but accurate language to go with all of the experiments, such as the exact names of the equipment.

Teach the correct names for plants, parts of the plants, and other terms as the chance arises. The correct names of plants in the environment should be given as the child learns to care for these things in the practical life work of the world of plants.

Just as with physics experiments, avoid giving simplified brief explanations when asked why something happens in the carrying out of an experiment.

Pre-reading Classified Pictures

This material helps increase the child's vocabulary and helps with classification of objects in his world. Here are some examples in the area of botany:

Plants

Trees

Wildflowers

Cultivated flowers

Classified Pictures Reading Stage or 3-Part Cards

Here is a partial list of some of the botanical subjects covered with this work for the primary, 3-6, class. I am putting them in the order that I introduced them in my own primary classes over the years:

Parts of

1. Parts of the plant: plant, root, stem, leaves, axis

2. Parts of the leaf: leaf, blade, margin, apex, base, stipule

3. Parts of the flower: flower, calyx, corolla, stamens, pistil

4. Parts of the root: root, root hairs, root cap, primary root, secondary root

5. Parts of the stem: stem, axil, nodes, axil bud, internode, and terminal bud

6. Parts of the bulb: bulb, stem, buds, fleshy leaves, roots, disc

7. Parts of the mushroom: mushroom, stalk, cuff, mycelium, spores, gills

Leaves

1. Leaf veins: parallel, reticulate

2. Leaf vein systems: main vein or midrib, side veins, veinlet

3. Leaves: simple or compound

4. Compound leaves: palmately compound, pinnately compound

5. Margins: palmately lobed, palmately fid, palmately partite, palmately sect

6. Margins: pinnately lobed, pinnately fid, pinnately partite, pinnately sect

7. Leaf shapes connected with geometry: ovate, obovate, cordate, obcordate, lanceolate, oblanceolate, hastate, sagittate, spatulate, reniform, elliptical, linear, acicular, orbicular, lyrate, runcinate, peltate

8. Leaf attachment to stem: petiolate, sessile

9. Leaf attachment to stem: opposite, alternate, whorled

(Note, learning about the stipule is important because that is how we figure out if we are holding in our hands a compound leaf or a stem with many leaves attached to it.)

10. Margins: entire or dented

11. Dented margins: serrate, dentate, or crenate

Flowers

1. Flower, types of corollas: rotate, tubular, hypocrateriform, more

2. Flower, parts of stamen: stamen, anther, filament, pollen

3. Flower, parts of pistil: pistil, ovary, style, stigma

4. Flower, types of sepals: polysepalous, gamosepalous

5. Flower, types of petals: gamopetalous, polypetalous

Roots

1. Types of roots: tap, fasciculated

2. Tap roots: tuberous, conical, napiform, and fusiform

Stems

1. Types of stem: subterranean (or underground), aerial

2. Stem: tuber, rhizome, bulb, and corm

3. Stem: Erect, climbing, and procumbent

4. Stem: woody, herbaceous, and shrubby

Buds

1. Types of buds: axil bud, terminal bud, flower bud, mixed bud (both flower and leaf)

Fruit

1. Fruits: succulent, dry

2. Types of succulent fruit: drupe (mango), berry (tomato), pepo (gourd, squash), pome (apple), hesperidium (orange), aggregate fruit (strawberry), syconus (fig)

3. Types of dry fruit: nut (chestnuts, acorns), legume (beans and peas), capsule (poppy, cotton), samara (maple seed), siligua (mustard)

Seeds

1. Parts of the seed: seed, testa, seed leaves, embryo, radicle, plumule

2. Types of seed leaves: monocotyledon, dicotyledon

The child should be introduced to live examples of these and have experienced as many examples and heard as many names as possible before being given the language material to read. These are all things that can be seen easily by a young child. At this age, unlike in the 6-12 class, we do not dissect! Children at this age naturally want to touch, smell, see, and learn to love nature, not to dissect it.

Pictures Showing "Parts of" in the Botany Area

You can see in the Classified Pictures Reading Stage list above that some of the selections for classified cards are also suitable for the "parts of" material. As always the real experience always comes before the label or language so before introducing this material to the child you will have had conversations about the parts of the leaf, flower, plant, etc.

Just as in the physics chapter you can present "Parts of" with a large picture of the whole object. On a large piece of cardboard the whole picture of a leaf could be drawn with no labels. The child places the labels, checking his work when he is finished by comparing his work with an identical large piece of card with the parts labeled.

Definition Reading Stages

These follow the list of Classified Pictures Reading Stage above.

FURTHER ACTIVITIES
IN THE WORLD OF BOTANY

Cutting and arranging flowers

In the winter, or whenever fresh flowers are not available, this can be done with stems of dried leaves or even just attractive stems so the child can make his flower arrangements from nature. This also helps the child develop a sensitivity to and appreciation for the shapes of plants and stems without leaves, and nature at all times of the year.

Pressing leaves and flowers

Just as dissecting flowers can sometimes be disturbing for the very young child, for an older child it is fine to press leaves and flowers.

Leaf collections

Older children can collect leaves. But help them stick to one classification at a time not just a random collection. For example a child can create a collection of a certain color of leaves in the fall, or tiny leaves instead of large ones, or collection by leaf shape, attachment to the stem, kinds of margins, simple or compound leaves.

Art

Children can make drawings or paintings looking at a living plant or flower, or from pictures in books

Art projects with leaves

Children at all ages can enjoy dipping a leaf in paint and using it to make designs on paper. Also putting a thin piece of paper over a leaf with large veins and coloring over it to transfer the vein pattern to the paper. An older child can do this with more delicate leaves and colored pencils when a lightness of touch is required. Leaves and flowers that have been pressed can be used to decorate other art projects such as that special birthday card for a friend or relative.

Planning a garden

This can be done, the children and adults working together, as different elements are taken into consideration, the color of the flowers, the height of the plant, the edging between the garden and the lawn, a rock garden, vegetables that can be used in the class, seasonal and local plant awareness, etc.

THE WORLD OF ZOOLOGY

From nowhere we came; into nowhere we go. What is life? It is the flash of a firefly in the night. It is the breath of a buffalo in the wintertime. It is the little shadow, which runs across the grass and loses itself in the sunset.

— Crowfoot, chief of the Blackfoot First Nation
in Canada 1890

Zoology is the study of animals. Teaching care of and compassion for animals can help children develop empathy for all living things, including their fellow human beings. And encouraging respect for animal habitats is an important part of teaching kids about protecting the environment. Having animals in the classroom—ideally as comfortable temporary guests who usually live in their natural environment rather than spending their lives in cages—gives children the chance to care for animals. It fosters in children an interest in learning more about animals and their needs. And it follows that they will become adults who care about preserving animal habitats as humans expand over the earth

In general there are two groups of animals that can be easily observed by children and so are appropriate to study at this age. These are vertebrates, or animals with backbones, and invertebrates, animals without backbones. Try to give the children the experience of both, but not at the same time.

Vertebrates

In the vertebrate area we include all five classes: Fish, amphibians, reptiles, birds, and mammals.

Fish are cold-blooded aquatic vertebrates usually having fins, gills, and a streamlined body. Try to find fish that are indigenous to your area. If you have an aquarium the size of the tank must be comfortable for the fish, not cruel. Try to create a balanced environment if these are pond fish, which means including snails, pondweed, and a piece of charcoal.

Amphibians are cold-blooded vertebrates that have an early aquatic stage and develop air-breathing lungs and usually 4 legs, as adults. The class of amphibians includes frogs, toads, newts, and salamanders. In the spring, bring in tadpoles and return them to the original pond when they turn into frogs.

Reptiles are cold-blooded vertebrates that have horny plates or scales. This class includes turtles, tortoises, crocodilians, snakes, and lizards. Bring in indigenous reptiles for just a short visit, as terrariums are difficult to maintain and keep healthy. Try to return them to the place where they were found after the visit.

Birds are warm-blooded, egg-laying, feathered vertebrates with forelimbs modified to form wings. To study birds it is best to have birdfeeders and maybe birdbaths — OUT OF REACH OF CATS — that can be seen from the classroom window, and cleaned and filled by the children (a wire brush to clean a stone birdbath for example).

Mammals are warm-blooded vertebrates that have hair and females with milk-producing glands. They give birth to life young. Some examples are visiting hamsters, gerbils, rabbits, rats, cats, etc. The mammal must be happy all during the visit.

Invertebrates

Here are some examples of invertebrates to study in the classroom:

Worms are very interesting creatures. A wormery can be as simple as a very large glass jar. Cover the glass with black paper so the worms will build their tunnels near the glass. Occasionally add more leaves or lettuce for food. Uncover the glass for a bit in order to see the worms up against the glass. After all of the children have seen them return the worms to the garden.

The same is true for ants; create a home filled with earth, sand, leaves, and ants. Cover the glass with black paper so the ants will build their tunnels near the glass. Uncover the glass to see the ants up against the glass. Commercial thin plastic worm homes filled with white sand are cruel. Only have them for a short period of time and return them to nature.

Butterfly and moth chrysalides and pupae are best observed in the garden. If they are in the classroom be sure you know what they need to hatch, and then return them to the wild. For example when a butterfly or moth emerges from a chrysalis the wings are soft and need to have room to hang down completely stretched out as they harden. So be sure there is a stick or something for the caterpillar to climb on.

Snails are very delicate and should be kept just for a day. Put a snail in a wide container on a piece of black paper to see his beautiful trail. Return it to the wild at the end of the day.

Live insects can be visitors in an insect-viewing container or a large glass bottle with a screen lid for a few hours. Take advantage of insects that wander into the classroom.

Be sure to protect these from sunlight in the classroom, as they are very delicate. For example do not put them in a window where afternoon sun could kill them.

PREPARING THE ENVIRONMENT

Have all of these materials clean, complete, in good repair. Keep language materials and books connected with these subjects in this area, sometimes placing a book or two in the book corner. As with the botany environment of course we must adapt to the conditions.

OUTSIDE ENVIRONMENT

Ideally there should be a small building or a place in the garden to keep animals. If this is not possible, then try to have healthy and comfortable places for animals inside. I saw a Montessori school for children from age 2 through high school in Colombia, South America, where farm animals are part of the outside environment so children from a very young age are able to observe them in their natural environment and learn to care for them.

INSIDE ENVIRONMENT

Have a place in the classroom for any equipment for classroom animals and visiting animals. Have a terrarium that can be quickly adapted to a visiting animal so the animal is comfortable and so it can be observed during its visit. Keep the animal food and other supplies here. Keep classified reading cards and books in this area.

Pictures for the Walls

Have beautiful pictures having to do with animals hanging on the walls at the eye level of the child. These can be a variety of photographs, reproductions of animals in great art such as depicted in oil paintings, prints, etchings, etc. Change them often.

Books

The animals in the books should not be anthropomorphized, or presented like humans that wear clothes and talk. This is something that is introduced later to teach more advanced life lessons. Examples of such books for older children who have learned the difference between reality and make-believe include stories about The Little Red Hen who had trouble getting anyone to grow grain and bake bread. Also Aesop's Fables. There are many books where animals act like people, but keep them for later. Children under the age of 5 are excited about learning about the real world.

Here are suggestions of the kinds of books related to the world of zoology that you might have in your classroom or home:

A book that contains clear pictures of the five classes of Vertebrates

Sea Fishes

Freshwater fishes

The Aquarium

Animals of Asia

Animals in the Deep Sea

The Book of the Coral Reef

Horses and Ponies

Mammals of the Desert Lands

Common Insects and Spiders

The Pond

Moths and Butterflies

Common Insects and Spiders

Birds Eggs

Cats

Mammals of Australia

Tropical Birds

Animals with shells

An Animal Picture Encyclopedia for Children

CARING FOR THE ZOOLOGY AREA

Caring for animals, and learning about their needs, is one of the most valuable ways a child can learn compassion. Following are some ideas of practical life exercises that can be provided that relate to taking care of the zoology area of the classroom. Before showing the child a lesson be sure that you practice it yourself, perhaps giving the lesson to another adult, so that it will be logical, clear, possible, for the child.

Taking Care of Animals

Feeding animals. Only capable children must do this. Feed the animals the proper food, in the proper amounts, at the correct times. The animals must come first.

Picking up and putting down an animal

Handling animals

Petting and grooming animals

Activities Related to Caring for Books and Equipment

Cleaning cages

Cleaning an aquarium

Cleaning feeding bowls and utensils

General techniques of handling books

Dusting and straightening shelves

A PERSONAL EXAMPLE

As in all areas we are sure that this is a useful, real example of important work that the child can manage. Then we analyze the steps and practice them before presenting the lesson to a child

Picking up a Kitten

Material: a kitten, perhaps in a box on the floor in front of you and the child

Presentation:

1. Lean slowly toward the kitten if possible making eye contact with the kitten.

2. Don't make any noise.

3. Place your left hand gently under the kitten's stomach.

4. Slowly move your right hand toward the kitten.

5. Place your right hand on the kitten's back.

6. Hold both hands gently in place for a moment.

7. Slowly lift the kitten from the box.

8. Do not squeeze but keep your hands relaxed.

9. Place the kitten gently on your lap.

10. If, during this sequence, the kitten starts to wiggle or fall, quickly but gently and quietly lower the kitten and settle him in the box.

Control of Error: The kitten. He will respond immediately if he is not picked up correctly, and settle nicely on your lap if handled correctly

Points of Consciousness:

1. The kitten should be in a receptive mood, not hungry, frightened, or sleeping, when this is attempted.

2. The child must have enough control not to squeeze the kitten.

3. The child must be able to remain calm and quiet.

4. He must be in control enough not to panic if the kitten tries to get away.

Purpose: To give the child practice in acting with consideration for an animal. Muscular control and concentration is practiced and refined. It gives practical information about handling a cat.

Age: Probably around 2.5 years, depending on the child.

SENSORIAL KEYS – THE ANIMALS

The animals themselves are the keys to the world of zoology. As a child observes animals with the senses of touch, sight, smell, sound, and learns their needs for comfort and food, the world of animals begins to be open to him. A sensorial key makes a connection in the mind of the child between one isolated characteristic of an animal, such as its size, the sound it makes, or skin covering, and the larger world of nature. These keys help the child want to explore further and make order of his world. They really are keys to the world.

Preparation for Animal Visitors

Always prepare ahead by learning what the visiting animal will need to be healthy, to get exercise, to eat and sleep. This includes animals that might be brought in just for one afternoon, or animals that will spend a few days in a prepared terrarium. The needs of the animal must come first.

Find out if the animals can be handled. Will they be observable (or are they always underground)? Do we have the food and water they need? If they are to stay longer will there be a place for them to be cared for during the holidays? What is the cost to keep an animal? Give the children as much information as possible before bringing an animal into the class. When the animal arrives encourage the children to observe its body and behavior.

Once the animal has arrived encourage a child, one or a small group at a time, to observe the animal, its body and behavior. Point out its features and offer a magnifying glass if the animal is small so the children will be able to observe in detail. Show the techniques for touching or handling an animal. You must establish rules about when and if the animal can be handled. Try to instill a respect about the necessity of providing as natural as possible an environment for animals as opposed to the environment that seems most comfortable to us.

Caring for an Animal

The adult puts out the amount of food that the animal needs just for one day so it will not be overfed. Eventually, after they realize the importance of not overfeeding, children can learn how much to give to the animal from the regular container. Feeding a fish or other animal must be considered a privilege.

Children must be shown how to hold an animal, and to understand that too much handling can make some animals sick. Holding an animal must be considered a privilege. Again, the needs and comfort of the animal must always come first.

NATURE WALKS

A walk in nature is another key to the world of zoology. For nature walks to experience insects, birds, and so on, stay near the premises and take only a few children at a time, moving at a very slow and calm pace. Just as in the classroom, do not interrupt careful observation and concentration by talking or moving a child on when he is not ready.

For nature walks off of the premises you will need several adults and it should be made clear who is in charge, taking responsibility for which children.

When you have a goal in mind for a nature walk, such as to observe birds' nests or parent birds feeding babies, find these things ahead of time so you are sure the children will be able to see them.

Because of the absorbent mind this child takes in all impressions of the world of animals. This means they will absorb our own attitude toward animals, effortlessly and completely, so be sure that you react to all animals in a positive and compassionate way.

These impressions become part of the child, forming his mind. Elements of the world of animals to which he is exposed now, both in the class and on nature walks, become very special to him later in life. This child will not need to be lectured about caring for the natural environment. It will be part of who he is.

LANGUAGE

(See the Language chapter for details and illustrations)

Stories

Learn to tell true stories to children about animals. For example I have told the story over and over about our horse getting out of the corral and looking in the window at the family one morning when we were all eating breakfast. It is a simple story with only a few sentences but the children asked for it over and over.

Vocabulary

Give the exact names for the animal, for example, not the generic word *cat* but Maine coon, tabby cat, Russian blue, Siamese, Manx, and so on. Even children in the Montessori infant communities for children from 1 to 2.5+ love to learn this kind of descriptive vocabulary. Teach the parts of animals, the needs of animals, and the food and equipment used in the zoology area.

There are three kinds of what we call card materials or language materials at this age. Pre-reading classified pictures, reading 3-part cards, pictures that illustrate clearly the various the parts of body of an animal, definition cards

Pre-reading Classified Pictures

This material helps increase the child's vocabulary and helps with classification of objects in his world. Here are some examples in the area of Zoology:

General Classifications of the Vertebrates

Fish

Amphibians

Reptiles

Birds

Mammals

Additions to these basic sets

Aquarium fish

Animals of the world

Animals of the continent where your children live

Animals of the children's own country

Animals grouped by climate such as desert, cold lands, jungle, etc.

Sets of different examples of the same animals (kinds of dogs, etc.)

Domestic animals

Wild animals

Farm animals

Sea mammals

Butterflies

Classified Pictures Reading Stage or 3-Part Cards

Three part cards can be made of any of the groups of animals in the above list. When the child has learned the names of these animals with the use of the pre-reading cards, he will be ready to test himself, and correct his own attempts by the use of 3-part cards.

The child should have been introduced to living animals first when possible, and should have heard as many names as possible before being given the language material to read. These are all things that can be seen easily by a young child. At this age, unlike in the 6-12 class, we do not dissect! Children at this age naturally want to touch, smell, see, and learn to love nature, not to dissect it.

Pictures Showing "Parts of" in the Zoology Area

Before introducing these picture cards to a child (each with just one part of the animal, such as head, foot, etc., colored in red) or perhaps at the same time, have a conversation about the parts of all of the different kinds of vertebrates, including humans. Then he will realize that vertebrates have some body parts in common; some have heads, most have legs, some have fins, and so on.

Just as in the physics and botany chapters you can present "Parts of" with a large picture of the whole object. On a large piece of cardboard the whole picture of a fish, for example, could be drawn with no labels. The child places the labels, checking his work when he is finished by comparing his work with an identical large piece of card with the parts labeled.

Here are examples of what is used for "parts of" language materials for vertebrates.

Fish: fish, head, caudal fin, pectoral fin, ventral fins, anal fin, dorsal fins, lateral line

Amphibian: frog, head, ear, body, forelegs, hind legs, foot

Reptile: tortoise, head, carapace, plastron, tail, claws

Bird: bird, head, beak, breast, wing, tail, legs, claws

Mammal: horse, head, ears, neck, mane, body, tail, hind legs, forelegs, hooves

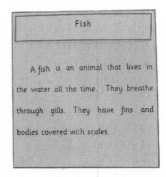

Fish

A fish is an animal that lives in the water all the time. They breathe through gills. They have fins and bodies covered with scales.

Definition Reading Stages

These follow the list of Classified Pictures Reading Stage above.

Be sure that the child has heard these definitions in conversations and perhaps had the definition booklets read to him before he is invited to read them. This is for the child that is just beginning to read sentences.

For the zoology area the definition booklets are made from the parts of the bodies above. There can also be definitions booklets that describe each of the classes of vertebrates, such as fish, amphibians, reptiles, birds, and mammals. And, assuming that the basics are covered, it is possible to go further for example definitions of invertebrates.

Further Activities
in the World of Zoology

Art

Children can be shown how to draw an animal by looking at the animal, or draw from the picture of an animal in a book. Seeing the world of zoology as created with original art by children has always been one of my favorite experiences as a teacher.

I will never forget the child in my primary class years ago that wanted to draw a picture of a toad that was visiting us for the day. He placed the large glass jar containing a bit of mud and some grass and the large toad on the table in front of him. Then he proceeded to carefully draw what he loved about this toad. The outline of the toad was definitely an abstract depiction, suggesting a head, body, and legs. But the spots! The hour of work was spent examining these spots in great detail and drawing each spot uniquely in its relative size, shape, and then colored with colored pencils. It was truly beautiful.

We never give adult-made outlines of animals for the children to fill in or work with in any way. We provide white paper, colored pencils and paints, and hopefully support that encourages the child in his desire to express himself. Providing adult-made animal outlines would give the message that the child's attempt at drawing is not good enough. The child's drawing is always better, more creative, interesting, and valuable.

Writing

Just as with the physics and botany experiments, if the older child wants to write about an animal he could write about what the visiting animal needed or what it looked like or acted like. Or he could write about an animal at home. Sometimes a child will combine a picture with a few words or sentences. Again, we provide only the paper and the respect for the child's way of expressing himself.

THE WORLD
OF GEOGRAPHY & HISTORY

Times have changed, and science has made great progress, and so has our work; but our principles have only been confirmed, and along with them our conviction that mankind can hope for a solution to its problems, among which the most urgent are those of peace and unity, only by turning its attention and energies to the discovery of the child and to the development of the great potentialities of the human personality in the course of its formation.

— Montessori, *The Discovery of the Child*

There are several direct aims of the geography and history part of the child's Montessori experience: to foster an interest in the physical environment of the world, to foster an interest in other people and other cultures, to foster an interest in events going on around us, and to begin to understand the fact that time passes and things change

We always keep in mind the fact that one rarely destroys what one loves, and the introduction of the world in this way prepares for a future where our planet and all kinds of people are understood and respected and loved.

Physical geography at this age deals with the way the earth is divided into land and water. It also introduces the child to the language or the names that humans have given to areas of both land and water: oceans, lakes, islands, and so on.

As the child learns about the earth he becomes interested in the places where land and water meet, interested in creating these land and water forms with clay or in the sandbox or at the beach, and then finding out and learning the names of these on maps of the earth and their own area of the world.

Cultural geography at this age introduces the idea that humans eat, dress, build their homes, and travel as a result of the climate where they live.

The child first experiences these things in his own home and in homes he visits, and with the clothing, the food, the transportation of his own family and friends. He is interested in facts and learning names or parts of the home, objects in the home, vehicles, clothing, and food. This naturally expands to include what other people in the world eat today, what they wear, how they travel and what their homes are like.

At the next stage of development, age 6-12, the child is more capable of abstract thought and analysis. At that age it is appropriate to explore the development of the mental and spiritual needs of humans throughout the ages and in many cultures. These include exploration, math, language, defense, religion, marriage, art, schools and education, and so forth. But for this age we stick to the physical needs, the sensorial exploration of food, homes, clothing, and transportation.

Learning to assemble the puzzle maps of the world, continents, countries, and local counties or areas, awakens an interest in other parts of the world. But this is not abstract thought about countries; it is to develop visual discrimination, eye-hand control, and memory, as the child learns to put together the puzzle map containing all of the countries of

Africa for example, by "absorbing" the relationships of these different shaped and colored puzzle pieces when the puzzle is assembled. Then he will be interested in learning the names of these pieces (countries) because he is familiar with the shapes, sizes, and colors, and because this is the time the child wants to know the names of everything. He is also interested in the colors and shapes and details of the flags of countries, the art, and music. These are all sensorial experiences appropriate to the age.

In learning about history, the child at this age cannot yet comprehend the reality of hundreds and thousands of years gone by. History at this age introduces the idea that things change as time passes, in his own life and in the world around him.

We must be careful not to turn this area into formal lessons on geography and history. Nothing is required but the children are presented with sensorial experiences and given the choice of what to work with. The focus in both geography and history is on objects and images, shapes and colors that can be experienced through the senses in the present moment.

This work lays the foundation for the way the human being explores from age seven on, when he will use his imagination to reach all over the earth, out into space, and to the past and the future.

PREPARING THE ENVIRONMENT

There should be a section of the classroom for the materials pertaining to humans and the world, including a wooden stand to hold the puzzle maps and a few shelves to hold the land and water forms, the flags, and the peoples of the world material, the globes, and the geography cards.

All of this material should be kept within easy reach of the children as an invitation for them to experience the material. Have all of these materials clean, complete, in good repair.

There should be a place on the wall for the Events Chart to be hung, and a news board if you have one in the classroom.

Pictures for the Walls

Have beautiful pictures of simple things in the natural and human world hanging on the walls. These are simple pictures hanging at the eye level of the child. They can be photographs and also examples, of clothing, food, vehicles, for example, from great art of the world. Change them often.

Books

Keep language materials and books connected with the physical world, peoples of the world, and history in this area sometimes placing one or two in the book corner. Have books and stories of events and personalities in history, and of the countries and peoples in the world. Be sure you have books that appeal to the very young child with interesting pictures, and also books with different levels of text for beginning and good readers. Read the book before deciding to offer it to a child, as there are many books of just facts that are intended for children but are not interesting to children.

There should be a children's picture atlas and other geography and history books. These may be kept in the geography and history area with a few related books placed in the book corner. Focus on the physical needs of humans and how they have been, or are, met. The other studies (religion, marriage, education, etc.) are more abstract and appropriate for later, children over age 7.

Here are some suggested subjects of books for this area of the environment:

Children's Picture atlas of the world

Books with pictures of lakes, mountains, rivers, etc.

Children's picture book of houses of the world

Same for clothing

Same for transportation

Same for foods of the world

Books of the child's culture showing clothing, shelter, food, and clothing

Books showing life in different climate zones, cold climate, Mediterranean climate, desert, and so on

Books each showing pictures of one particular country

Books showing the past of the child's own country

Books on famous people of the child's own country

Books with pictures of civilizations of the past – but emphasizing shelter, foods, clothing, and transportation (the physical needs of humans)

CARING FOR THE GEOGRAPHY & HISTORY AREA

Following are some ideas of practical life exercises that can be provided that relate to taking care of the geography and history area of the classroom. Before showing the child a lesson be sure that you practice it yourself, perhaps giving the lesson to another adult, so that it will be logical, clear, possible, for the child.

Carrying a flag on the open palm while *walking on the line* (see glossary)

Pouring water into the land and water models

Dusting puzzle maps and globes

Dusting and straightening shelves

Polishing puzzle maps

Carrying puzzle maps correctly

Cleaning up materials used in art work connected with this area

Correct handling, carrying, carrying for books and language materials

Placing the pins in the pin maps

A PERSONAL EXAMPLE

As in all areas we are sure that this is a useful, real example of important work that the child can manage. Then we analyze the steps and practice them before presenting the lesson to a child.

Carrying a Puzzle Map

Material: a large Montessori puzzle map of the continents of the world, the one presented first. The puzzle map is either in the map cabinet or on a shelf. The child has already placed his floor mat on the floor ready for this lesson.

Presentation:

1. Stretch out both arms toward the puzzle map in front of you.

2. Place one hand on each side of the puzzle map, slowly moving our hands from near the front to toward the middle of the sides of the puzzle map.

3. Grasp the map firmly with both hands.

4. Lift the map slowly, holding it so that the edge closest to you is firm against your body and the puzzle map is horizontal, not tilted.

5. Look in the direction that you want to walk, making sure that no one is in your way.

6. Walk slowly toward the floor mat, holding the puzzle map exactly as described in step 4.

7. Be careful not to bump into anyone or anything. If someone is in your way stop walking and wait patiently.

8. Lower the map slowly onto the floor mat.

9. Let go of it.

Control of Error:

The puzzle map will not be dropped and you will not bump into anyone if it is transported correctly.

Points of Consciousness:

1. The child must be strong enough to carry the puzzle map. Children, as soon as they learn to walk, want and need to be given the opportunity to carry heavy things by themselves. Do not present this to two children to carry together. This is cumbersome and it requires a child to interrupt someone else in his or her work to ask for help. As long as the child is strong enough, carrying the puzzle map alone is important for physical and psychological reasons, and an important step in developing independence in action and thought.

2. The child must be able to grasp the puzzle map in the middle of the sides. This can mean slowly and incrementally removing it from the map stand if this is used.

3. The child must already know how to walk across the room without bumping into things or stepping on floor mats WITHOUT the map before he can do it carrying the puzzle map.

Purpose: The child gains the independence of being able to work on this large piece of material without the aid of the teacher or another child. This is an exercise in control of movement.

Age: 1.5 – 3 on

Land and Water Forms

Materials:

Eight trays in which these land and water forms are represented: island, lake, cape, bay, peninsula, gulf, isthmus, and strait

These are commercially available but I never used such versions because there is very little to challenge a child who just pours water in forms made by someone else. I have always made my own, and invited the children to make their own, out of plasticine or clay. This is more interesting because, as he learns from exploring globes and maps, there are many different variations of all land and water formations.

Here is the description in case you also want to make your own. Eight metal trays, 8 inches square and 2 inches tall. I have also used small stainless steel individual pie pans. If you like you can paint the pans blue to represent the water. Make the land and water forms with real clay and, when dried, paint the clay green to represent the land.

Aim: This provides a sensorial introduction and experience with the land and water forms.

Presentation:

Everything kept out on a table with a pitcher, cloth, and floor cloth. If using premade forms the young child is invited to feel them, pour water into them, empty and dry them thoroughly. After a lot of experience with them, teach the child the names of them and link them up to the land and water cards.

Point of Consciousness:

The land and water forms can be presented all at once, all of them on a table at the same time. But if you do not have room they can be presented in pairs, as mirror images of each other. For example an island is a piece of land completely surrounded by water and a lake is a body of water completely surrounded by land. This is true for cape-bay, peninsula-gulf, and strait-isthmus. This is another valuable classification.

Age: approximately 3 years for premade forms, later for making one's own

Globe Showing Land and Water

Material: A globe of the world, the surface of the land is made of sandpaper and the area representing water is painted blue.

Aim: To give a sensorial impression of the world's land and water areas and to introduce the idea that our world is divided into land masses and stretches of water.

Presentation:

1. To prepare for feeling the sandpaper areas of this globe, sensitize your fingers by dipping in warm water and rubbing with a cloth, invite the child to do the same.

2. Take the globe to a floor mat or tablemat.

3. Feel the globe dramatically, casually giving the names Earth, land, and water, as you draw the child's attention to every detail, even the tiniest bits of land and water.

4. Invite the child to do the same.

Age: approximately 3 years

Globe with the Continents in Color

It is with the following work that the child moves from purely a physical geography way of learn about the Earth (land and water) to the geo-political way of looking at Earth because of the presence of humans. This will go on with all of the work of humans to define boundaries and give names. At this age it is a sensorial exploration and at the 6-12 level the studies will be go deep into the history of this development.

Material:

The land and water globe

The globe, the same size, with the globe (no sandpaper) with the continents painted in color

Aim: To show that the land on Earth is divided into continents and to give a sensorial impression of the continents of the world

Presentation:

1. Take both globes to a floor mat or tablemat.

2. Tell the child that these are the same earth, pointing out the continents on both.

3. Point out a continent on the colored globe and invite the child to find it on the land and water globe.

4. As he is doing this casually mention the names of the continents: Asia, Africa, North America, South America, Australia, Antarctica, and Europe.

5. Explore the globe with the child, showing the child's own continent, talking about the colors, and so forth

5. Leave the child to explore both globes on his own.

Age: around 3 years, almost immediately after you have introduced the land and water globe.

Note: Do not go further into the various ways of defining continents, as this is a subject for the history of geography studied at the elementary, age 6-12, level. This is a sensorial beginning for the child to classify impressions.

Knobbed Puzzle Maps

Material:

A cabinet containing knobbed wooden puzzle maps, in this order beginning at the top:

The world/continents

The child's continent

The child's country if there is such made (The picture above is of the country of Russia.)

The child's own region or state if available

The other continent puzzle maps

Note: The knobs are placed where the capital of a country is. For the child's continent the knobs are placed where the capital of the state or area is. For example the knob for lifting the puzzle piece for the state of California is where the capital, Sacramento, is.

Aims:

1. To give the child a sensorial impression of the world, the continents, particularly his own country.

2. To help the child orient himself on the planet earth sensorially.

3. To link the concept of the continents on the colored globe with that represented on a 2-dimensional map.

4. Indirectly the knobs support the development of the hand and fingers for writing

Presentation 1:

1. Take the continent, the first puzzle map, to a floor map. Be sure to model the correct way to carry the puzzle map. Even the youngest child wants to, and is able, to carry the large puzzle maps alone. Place it carefully on one side of the floor mat.

2. Remove one or two pieces and soundlessly place them back where they belong.

3. Remove out one or two different pieces and again, soundlessly, replace them.

4. Invite the child to have a turn.

5. Gradually increase the number of pieces to be removed at a time.

6. Remove all of the pieces and put them back.

Presentation 2:

1. Show the child how to remove the pieces and mix them up (we called this "making a muddle" in my training in London) and then put them back.

Presentation 3:

Show the child how to remove the pieces and recreate the way they are arranged in the puzzle map, but this time on the floor mat. First this is done piece by piece, and eventually by mixing the pieces and then assembling them on the floor map

Presentation 4:

Go through these stages with other puzzle maps, first the child's continent and then his country, and then other continents.

Control of Error: The control is visual, that the puzzle maps are put together the way they were when they were first removed from the map cabinet.

Language: After the child has worked with several maps, begin to teach him the names of the pieces by means of the three-period lesson (see glossary for this lesson)

Age: approximately 3 years, begin after the child has explored the globe with the continents in color.

Peoples of the World

Material:

This material presents several scenes resembling miniature theatre scenes, each representing a different climate area of the world.

Each set contains:

1. A backdrop that stands up that shows what the area of the world looks like

2. Standing models of people and objects such as types of transportation, animals, different family members, examples of homes and so forth

Aims:

To offer the perspective that people have different homes, clothing, foods, and transportation dictated by the climate in which they live.

To spark the child's interest in learning more about the world

Presentation 1:

1. Have the child help you remove one set from the box or container in which it is kept and set it up. Discuss the contents.

2. Introduce the standing models (people, animals, transportation, etc.) one at a time, discussing each and placing them in the scene, in front of the backdrop.

3. Tell the child as much as possible about the life of the people who live in such a place. This should be an interesting but non-fictional story.

4. Leave the child to work with the scene on his own.

Presentation 2: The child can take out two sets and set them both up and compare. For example the figures of people dressed for life in a tropical jungle would not be comfortable in front of the scene white with snow from cold lands. Gradually increase the number of sets the child can explore, compare, and assemble, at a time.

Age: approximately 4 years.

Note: Because creating these materials is time consuming many teachers have begun to make continent folders of pictures or continent boxes. These are interesting but they can be confusing to children because there are so many different cultures and climate zones on each continent. It is more valuable to create the Peoples of the World climate zone material.

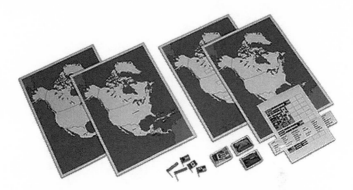

Pin Maps

Materials:

A set of 4 wooden maps of the child's continent

1: The first map is blank, no countries or capitals labeled. There are three holes in each country. The hole for the pin identifying the capital of that country is outlined with a narrow strip of red. This hole is in the same spot where the capital of the country is.

2. The second map has the names of the countries (there are no holes)

3. The third map has the names of the capitals (there are no holes)

4. The fourth map has small pictures of the flags of each country (there are no holes)

A box of pins each with a green label and the name of one of the countries of the continent

A box of pins each with a red labels and the name of the capital of one of the countries of the continent

A box pins each with a flag of one of countries of that continent attached.

Aim: To introduce the child to the geographical names and the flags of all of the countries of his continent.

Presentation 1 - Names of the Countries Map:

1. Have the child take maps 1 (the blank map) and 2 (with the names of the countries) and the box of pins with green labels each with the name of a country to a table or a floor mat.

2. Introduce map 2 and with the child read some of the names of the countries he has already learned with the knobbed puzzle maps of his continent. Then put this map out of the way or turn it over and explain that we will use it later

3. Place the blank map in front of the two of you.

3. Show him the pins with green labels giving the names of the countries and together lay them out in columns next to the blank map, reading them as you do so.

4. Choose one of the green labels, have a child read it and find the country on map 1.

5. Have him place the label on the appropriate country. Be sure to explain that it can go in any hole except for the one with the red outline.

6. When he is finished show him that he can check his work by comparing it with map 2 that has the names of all of the countries.

Presentation 2 - Names of the Capitals Map:

Present this exactly as you have the names of the countries except this time you use map 1 (the blank map), map 3 (the map with the names of the capitals), and the red labels.

Explain that a capital is a city where the head of the government is located. Be sure to show him that these pins with the red labels go in the holes that are outlined in red.

If this is the first introduction to the names of the capitals the child might need to look at map 3 at first as he places the pins in the correct holes. But he will probably, at this age, want to be able to place all of the capitals without looking and then use map 3 as his own control of error.

Presentation 3 - Flag Map:

Present this in the same way as with Names of the Capitals but using maps 1 and 4

Age: 4.5 year and older, when the child can read and is interested in learning to read new words

Note: Because of the small pins, which children love to carefully handle and place, companies that make these materials are protecting themselves by labeling them for age 7 and up. This is sensorial/language material appropriate, and originally created for, the primary class.

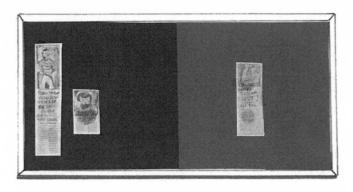

HISTORY

At this age a simple concept of present and past is given in two ways. The first is the Events Chart that introduces the concept of present and past. The second is the Personal Time Line that shows the child that his own life is made up of the present and the past.

Events Chart

Material:

A bulletin board divided into left and right halves. It can be described as present and past later with the children, or you can label the two halves.

Newspaper or magazine clippings, or items printed from the Internet, about an on-going event or related series of events that children would be hearing about in their day-to-day lives

Aim: To show the relationship between past and present, how the present becomes the past.

An indirect aim is that of preparing for timelines that the child will see and work with later in life.

Presentation:

1. Choose a topic that will interest the children.

2. Collect labeled and described pictures illustrating the topic, from newspaper, magazine, or the Internet, and encourage children to bring them in from home.

3. Tack one or two of these pictures on the part of the board that is labeled "present".

4. Discuss the event and pictures with the children.

5. After a week or two select some more recent pictures about this topic.

6. Remove the first pictures from the "present" section and move them to the "past" section.

7. Put the new clippings on the "present" side.

8. Explain what you are doing to the children. These things are happening now, in the present. These have already happened in the past.

9. Do this weekly if possible. Eventually change the topic.

Age: 3 years and older

Note: In Thailand I have seen elementary-type timelines of the evolution of plants and animals on Earth that began on the right side and moved to the left. This made me think that it is arbitrary that we move from left to right as we study past to present. I have also seen these timelines that are vertical and move from bottom to top or even top to bottom. So make the present and past in your classroom the same of any expression of the passage of time in your own culture.

1 year   SUSAN KOW was born in HONG KONG

2 years   I stepped on a nail and went to the hospital

3 years   my birthday party

4 years   when I was 4 I came to San Francisco

5 years

Personal Timeline

Materials:

A long, narrow piece of paper or cardboard divided into 4, 5, 6 sections depending on the age of the child, each section representing a year in the child's life. There should be different colors on the edge of the timeline, each color representing one year.

Get pictures of the child at birth and during each of these years ahead of time.

Aim: To give the child a further understanding of the passage of time.

Presentation:

Help the child create his timeline, coloring the sides of each year a different color, and placing the pictures in the appropriate year.

Write a fact from each year that you have learned from the parents. Or you can ask the child what he wants to say about each picture.

Further Activity:

If a child gets very involved with the making of his own time lines he could also make timelines of his parents, siblings, and friends. The child can make his drawings rather than using real photographs if he desires.

Age: at least old enough to be able to do this work, and to have 4-6 years represented

Note: This is not something that is done at the end of the child's primary class experience as an expected tradition, nor is it something made for celebrating a birthday. There is usually an example for children to look at on the history/geography area of the classroom and then it is a choice given to the child just as any other project connected with the cultural areas.

LANGUAGE

(See the Language chapter for details and illustrations)

Land & Water Form Cards, Pre-reading Classified Pictures

This material helps increase the child's vocabulary and helps with classification of objects in his world. Here are some examples in the area of Geography:

Unlabeled pictures of each of the land and water forms. They should be created in pairs for example the island and lake the same shape just the colors reversed. The island is green and the surrounding water blue. The lake is blue and the surrounding land green.

In this case the classified pictures will be shown with the land and water forms, and the teacher will casually use the words of the definitions in talking about them to the child.

Classified Pictures Reading Stage or 3-Part Cards

Three part cards can be made of all eight of the land and water forms. When the child has learned the names of with the use of the pre-reading cards, he will be ready to test himself, and correct his own attempts by the use of 3-part cards.

Definition Reading Stages

These follow the list of Classified Pictures Reading Stage above.

Be sure that the child has heard these definitions in conversations and perhaps had the definition booklets read to him before he is invited to read them.

Here are definitions appropriate for a child to learn at this age:

A *lake* is an extensive sheet of water enclosed by land, occupying a hollow in the earth's surface.

An *island* is a piece of land entirely surrounded by water.

A *gulf* is a deep inlet of water almost surrounded by land, with a narrow mouth.

A *peninsula* is a piece of land almost surrounded by water or projecting out into a body of water.

A *strait* is a narrow stretch of water connecting two extensive areas of water.

An *isthmus* is a narrow strip of land with water on either side, forming a link between two larger areas of land.

A *cape* is a rounded or more or less pointed piece of land jutting out into a body of water.

A *bay* is a broad sheet of water jutting into land.

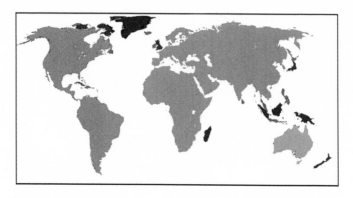

Language Maps

Material, an example Islands of the World:

1. A globe, either one of those described above, or a classroom political globe

2. An "Islands of the World" chart, perhaps 11" x 14" or larger, with an outline map of the world and with perhaps the ten largest islands of the world colored, all the same color, and labeled

3. A second chart exactly the same, islands colored the same but not labeled

4. Little cards with the labels written on them

Presentation:

1. Show the child the globe and help him find some islands. Since he might know the definition of "island" by this time point out that several continents are islands. If this happens tell him that even though some of the continents are really islands, for our purposes we are going to look for other

islands. (In academic circles, a body of land can be called either a continent or an island, not both.)

2. Show him the labeled chart. Read the labels with him and then find those islands on the globe.

3. Turn over the chart with the labels and show him the unlabeled chart.

4. After doing one or two yourself invite the child to place the labels where he thinks they go.

5. Show him how to turn over the labeled chart to check his work.

Variations 1:

Create the same kind of language maps to teach the major lakes, capes, bays, and the other land and water forms of the world. Also you can make maps showing the oceans or seas of the world.

Variations 2:

Create the same kind of language maps to teach the major land and water forms of the child's continent, and then the child's country, and then state.

Aims:

To learn the names of the land and water forms of the world and the child's area of the world

To inspire interest in learning more about Earth

Control of Error: the maps with names

Age: when the child has learned all about land and water forms and is beginning to read

FURTHER ACTIVITIES IN THE WORLD
OF GEOGRAPHY AND HISTORY

Drawing and Painting Maps

Just as with other art, drawing from life or from pictures in books, children can learn to look at a puzzle piece of a continent or country or state and draw it freehand. Then he can paint it. Drawing freehand should always be encouraged.

Map Collage

The child can draw around a puzzle piece of a continent or countries on colored paper, cut it out, and reconstruct his own map by pasting it on white paper

Drawing and Painting Flags

This should also be done freehand and not with adult-created outlines. Children can just paint freehand, or draw and then fill in with colored pencil, paint, or even create with collage, the map of the child's choice. This is most successfully done if the child has the large maps that are often found in a Montessori classroom and with a full-size piece of white paper for each flag.

Making Advanced Maps

Older children can make their own maps with the names of a country, the capital in the correct place, and flags – inspired by work with the pin maps.

Peoples of the World

Children can make their own backdrops and scenes inspired by the peoples of the world material, or draw, paint, label, or write about this subject.

THE WORLD OF MUSIC

M*usical ability is not an inborn talent but an ability, which can be developed. Any child who is properly trained can develop musical ability just as all children develop the ability to speak their mother tongue. The potential of every child is unlimited.*

—Shinichi Suzuki

Music begins before birth as the child listens to the voices and music around him. A song sung to him during this time has been known to calm him after birth. In today's busy and loud world it is important to realize that the young child hears everything without being able to block out sound. So attention to sounds and music is very important in our classes. For example there should not be constant "background" music. An adult will learn not to hear but at this age a child cannot block it out and it can affect everything he does interrupting his concentration.

Because of the importance of the uninterrupted 3-hour work period, music in the Montessori primary class is not a scheduled whole-group activity. The teacher may gather a small group of children who are in-between other activities and present one of the music activities, ask a child to select a song card and then sing with the group, play a piano or guitar and sing with the children, or work with the language materials, but these are spontaneous, unscheduled activities.

Children are also free to do any of these things alone or with a friend at any time.

During my first AMI teacher training course in London this approach was brought to my attention in a delightful way. I was observing a class where everyone was very busy and concentrating. I saw a child go up to the teacher and whisper something in her ears. Together they went over to a tape player (cassette tapes were precursors of the CD's we use today) and look through several, the child choosing one, and then placing it in the machine.

Next they made a larger floor space by moving a few chairs out of the way. Then they both sat down on a chair, removed their "inside" shoes and placed them neatly under the chairs. Now, in stocking feet, they crossed the open space and pushed the button to pay the music.

Together they listened to the music and danced, moving their bodies and swaying their arms intently as they listened to the rhythms coming from the tape player. The teacher of course paid attention to the child's interest and it was the child who stopped dancing first. Then together they took the tape out of the machine, replaced it in its folder, put on their inside shoes and put the chairs back where they had been.

What struck me most of all is that no one seemed to notice what they were doing! Everyone had continued to concentrate on his or her own work as the dancing was happening. No one looked up or seemed at all disturbed by the music or the activity. This showed me that it was an isolated activity but a non-scheduled, child-chosen activity that was typical of the way music was experienced in this class.

Just as "walking on the line" gives a child the opportunity to focus on moving his feet slowly and with focus and concentration, moving to music as described provides the best experience for responding to different kinds of rhythms and pitches. Carefully listening and responding by moving one's body is an instinct that has been valuable for thousands of years and it begins with the very young child.

Through the music activities that will be described in this session the children learn to experience, explore, and classify the elements of music such as rhythm, pitch, timbre, intensity, and moving to music. They learn to arrange and perform music concerts for their friends.

They learn to respect and handle carefully musical instruments, and to learn the names of these instruments and composers. They learn to identify by listening to the musical instruments as well as the music of composers and music from different ethnic traditions.

Learning to create music and then interpret the music created by others parallels that of the development of language.

First the child listens and organizes spoken language in his own mind. Then he practices making the sounds of language, gradually and naturally learning to use the correct structure of sentences, "music" of language, and then to express himself by means of all of these skills he has absorbed since birth. After all of this he learns to "write" words that he is thinking in his own mind, and only later to read words that have been written down by someone else.

In music it is the same. A child can certainly have a head start when he is still in the womb if one of the parents is a musician practicing on a cello or piano several hours a day, or a lover of music who sings or plays an instrument almost every day. If this has not been the case then we must be aware of our own responsibility to provide live music by playing an instrument ourselves or bringing in visiting musicians, and by offering the very best quality of music CDs for a child to select at any time and listen to usually in a quiet corner of the room.

Through the sensorial keys of musical activities the child begins to discover the variety of possibilities by expressing music through the voice and with a variety of percussion instruments.

Most of all, music is a way to experience and express all of the emotions known to humans. And in the Montessori class, where it is common that children experience happiness, it is often expressed by spontaneously beginning to sing, even when concentrating on something else. I have often observed this and have the satisfying feeling that in my small circle of humanity, "All is right with the world."

PREPARING THE ENVIRONMENT

There should be a section of the classroom where the materials pertaining to music are kept together. The CD player, percussion instruments, the Montessori bells if you have them, and language materials and books. All of the music materials should be kept clean and in good repair as should the shelves where they are kept.

A CD player can be adapted so that the volume is kept low enough for the person sitting next to it to hear well and it is not disturbing to children working far across the room. Earphones are NOT used in the Montessori classroom for several reasons; we do not know yet the far-reaching effects of such things on the delicate ears of a young child, and emotionally the use of earphones turns a person inward for pleasure rather than to the society of others. These are two very important reasons.

Have a well-thought out selection of CDs for the children to experience.

The percussion instruments are of the best quality possible, not toys, and ideally represent a variety of cultures. For example Maracas from Latin American, finger cymbals from the Middle Eastern belly dancing tradition, ankle bells used in classical Indian dancing, a small but real djembe drum from Africa, and so on.

Show the children how to pick up, carefully put down, and handle the instruments before using them. You can point out something about each instrument such as where the name came from, or the country or what the instrument is made of. After an instrument has been played give the name.

Pictures for the Walls

Have beautiful pictures of musical instruments, composers, or of people making music, perhaps nicely framed or presented reproductions of great art throughout the world, people dancing or playing music. These pictures are hung so that the center of the image is level with the eye level of the average aged child. Change the pictures often so they will continue to attract the attention of the children.

Books

Keep language materials and books connected with music in this area, sometimes placing one or two in the book corner.

Be sure you have books that appeal to the very young child with interesting pictures, and also books with different levels of text for beginning and good readers. Read the book before deciding to offer it to a child, as there are many books of just facts that are intended for children but are not interesting to children.

Here are some suggestions of topics for books in the music area of the classroom or for the home:

A picture book of the history of music

A picture book of musical instruments

Books about ballet and other kinds of dancing

Sometimes there are good children's books about individual composers

Books about music in various countries

CARING FOR THE MUSIC AREA

Activities related to caring for music equipment and also books and related equipment:

Carrying chair to clear a space for dancing

Carrying a chair to clear a space for a small group activity

Handling the CD player

Handling the CDs

Carrying and handling percussion instruments

Playing a percussion instrument correctly

Picking up, carrying, putting down the Montessori bells

Correctly striking the bell striker and damper

Dusting or cleaning the music equipment and shelves

Handling the music pictures and books

A Personal Example

As in all areas we make sure that this is a useful, real example of important work that the child can manage. Then we analyze the steps and practice them before presenting the lesson to a child

Playing a Triangle

Material: a metal Triangle held by a string and beater kept on a tray or in a small basket

Presentation 1:

1. Gently pick up the triangle by the string keeping your fingers in an "o" shape.

2. Move the triangle to in front of you just below eye-level about a foot away from your face, emphasizing that it is not touching anything.

3. Gently pick up the beater holding it carefully by the handle on one end.

4. Hold the beater a few inches from the triangle at a 45-degree angle.

5. Gently strike the triangle on the outside of one of the three sides.

6. Hold still and wait, listening till the sound fades away.

7. Replace the triangle and beater to the tray or basket and invite the child to do the same.

8. Depending on the attention of the child, at some point give the names "triangle" and "beater."

Presentation 2:

When a child is skilled at the above show him how to dampen the sound. This takes coordination because the beater must be held in such a way that the index finger is free.

1. As in the first presentation.

2. After step 5 above, as the triangle is sounding, gently touch the triangle with the index finger. The sound will be stopped.

3. Give the language, "The sound has been dampened."

Presentation 3:

When the child knows how to use the triangle correctly and dampen the sound you can show them the 2-sided triangle roll.

1. Hold the beater inside of the triangle, near one of the corners.

2. With great attention gently strike one side of the triangle near this corner, then the other side, then moving back and forth between two sides. Striking near the corners makes a more gentle sound. Experiment.

3. Wait for the sound to go away.

4. Combine this with use of the damper if possible.

3. The language is, "a 2-sided triangle roll."

Presentation 4:

1. As above strike one side of the triangle, but this time strike in the middle of the side instead of near the corner.

2. After striking this side of the triangle, strike the middle of the second side.

3. Then strike the middle of the third side.

4. Continue to strike each of the sides in order two or three times, rotating in a kind of circle within the triangle.

5. Listen as the sound fades away after the last strike.

6. Next time dampen the triangle as above after the last strike.

7. The language is, "a 3-sided triangle roll."

Points of Consciousness:

1. These last two presentations must be taught very carefully, with great attention, to a child who is skilled and ready for them. They should not be license to wildly strike a triangle without intention.

2. These are the same steps that a university percussion student or professional musician learns in order to play this instrument in an orchestra.

3. Be sure that you can do all of the above well before showing a child

4. The triangle must be of good quality, not a toy, in order to get a beautiful sound

Purpose:

To aid in developing muscular control and concentration. Eye-hand coordination is refined. It teaches respect for musical instruments. The skill in hearing is improved.

Age: Approximately 3 for the first presentation, depending on the child's coordination.

Sensorial Keys

Musicians, Musical Instruments and Music Activities, Recorded Music, and the Montessori Bells

VISITING MUSICIANS

It is important for children to learn that the movement of a human body, not just what they would hear on the radio, makes music. When you invite musicians to come and show their instruments to the children keep these two things in mind:

1 - Explain that you only want the musician to play for five minutes or so, leaving the children curious and wanting to know more about the instrument, not overwhelmed. Suggest that the musician take just a few moments, not a lecture as would be given to adults, to show and name the parts of the violin so the children know where the sound comes from.

2 - Explain to the musician that after hearing him play you would like the children to be able to gently touch the instrument so they can experience it with as many senses as possible. Of course the musician should show how this is done.

Following the visit, link the experience with the rest of the music area. For example if a musician is going to show the children a violin, you might have hung a picture of a violin in the music area ahead of time, and made sure that a CD of violin music, and the language materials showing the parts of the violin, are all presently on the shelves. Hearing even a few moments of a real violin being played by a person, and seeing the beauty of the wood, and seeing all of the parts of the violin and perhaps being allowed to gently touch it, will make all of these other connected experiences much more interesting and enjoyable.

After I had taught primary classes for several years, I took the AMI elementary teacher training for children in 6-12 classes. Sanford Jones, professional pianist and musician of children's opera fame and Montessori elementary teacher, gave the lectures on music. Before giving us the lessons for the elementary class he gave an overview of what he had done, sensorially, in the primary music area before the more abstract work in the elementary class.

MUSICAL INSTRUMENTS
AND MUSIC ACTIVITIES

The following "music activities" were part of his primary overview. Since then I have done them in several elementary classes, in one primary class, and I have taught them to many adults. They add a lot to the child's ability to explore and classify the elements of music and they make a child curious and wanting to know more about music.

These lessons involve the hands, the whole body, and the voice. As with all Montessori lessons, there are times when lessons are given to groups.

When beginning a new class, before children learn to work individually, many lessons are given as group presentations. When two or three children are between projects and have not decided what to choose to work on next this is a good time to gather a small group. And for some of the music exercises a small group is required. Eventually, just as with all of the primary class work, children will initiate these activities on their own and do them alone or with a few friends.

Rhythm - Heartbeat "Pulse"

Ask a child to find his heartbeat by feeling for it on his neck or wrist, and then nod his head when he feels each beat. The teacher matches the nodding head by tapping a drum or tambourine. Now ask the child to run in place for a few seconds. The heartbeat will speed up. Again match the feeling of the heartbeat with the tapping of the percussion instruments and tell the child that the "pulse" is faster. Point out that if we want to sleep we would want a slower pulse. Sometimes there is a faster pulse sometimes a slower pulse in music.

Rhythm - Matching a Pulse

Sing bits of a song (or play on piano or guitar if the teacher plays these instruments), and have the child match the pulse by tapping on his knees.

Rhythm of Children's Names

You will need at least 3 children for this lesson. Ask each child in turn to say his name (at first just first name, then whole name). Match the rhythm by tapping it out on the instrument, "Susan" (one loud tap, one soft tap), "Alexander" (two soft taps, one loud tap, one soft tap). Then ask the children to stand up, and move a bit away facing the other direction. Tell them to return and sit down when they hear their name. Tap out each name on the instrument.

Rhythm - Stepping to the Rhythm of a Musical Phrase

Have a child take tiny steps (NOT on the line) as you sing each syllable. Good examples are "twinkle, twinkle, little star, how I wonder how you are. The child will take 7 tiny steps and then pause at "star" and "are".

Rhythm - Conducting Forms

Most music moves in groups of 2, 3, or 4 beats. This is a more advanced lesson but you might be able to do it. Play or sing three songs as examples of each. Here are three examples, the first two songs that Sanford Jones wrote:

Alleluia – 2 beats

Sunflower – 3 beats

Are You Sleeping – 4 beats

Show these casually on other songs over a period of time.

Then introduce the way a conductor would move his arms. Up and down for 2 beats, in a triangle for 3 beats, and a square for 4 beats.

Have the child move his arms in these ways as he listens to music.

Cardboard conductor shapes can be created, or have a child draw these shapes on a piece of paper and point to them as another person sings a song.

Musical Pitches Experienced with the Body

You are going to play the pitches on a piano, or a guitar.

Tell the child that when he hears a high "pitch" he should reach up and pretend that he is picking cherries from high up in a tree (or whatever is culturally familiar).

When he hears a low pitch he should reach down near the floor as though picking strawberries.

And for middle pitch reach out in front and pick blueberries.

Demonstrate and give the words, high pitch, low pitch, and middle pitch.

Pitch - Finishing a Musical Phrase

Sing part of a song and ask the child to give the missing word at the correct pitch. Example "twinkle, twinkle, little _____" (filling in the last word at the correct pitch) or "twinkle, twinkle _____ _____" (filling in the last two words at the correct pitch)

Timbre of Percussion Instruments

Be sure the child knows the names of the percussion instruments before this lesson. Have him close his eyes. Then as you tap each instrument ask the child to tell you which one is being played.

Timbre of the Human Voice

Again this is a lesson for a small group. Ask for a volunteer, one child to close his eyes and guess who is going to be speaking. Tell him to say the name of whoever is speaking.

Whisper into the ear of each of the children who are going to speak, "When I point to you say 'Today is Tuesday' " (or pick any phrase).

Then, with the volunteer's eyes still closed, point to a child. He speaks. The child with closed eyes guesses who it is.

Do this until everyone has been identified by voice.

Tell the children that the reason they knew who was speaking was because the voice of each person had a specific timbre.

Note: Both of the above timbre games can be done at a distance for more refinement of awareness of sound.

Timbre of Sounds in the Environment

Have a child, or each child in a small group, close his eyes for a short period of time and listen to the sounds in the inside or outside environment. You could mark the length of time with a bell. At the end of the period ask him to name some of the sounds he hears. You can explain that he knew what was making the sound because he recognized the timbre.

Intensity of Loud and Soft Tapping

Demonstrate the difference between loud and soft by tapping knees or a drum while singing. As you tap loudly, the children and you will automatically sing louder. As you tap softly you all will automatically sing more softly. Then you can lead by tapping loudly or softly and have the children join you with clapping. Use the words *loud* and *soft*.

Intensity - *Piano* and *Forte*

After some experiences using the words loud and soft, you can explain that in music we use the Italian word *piano* when we want music to be played softly, and the Italian word *forte* when we want it to be played loudly. If the children get this very quickly you can challenge them to express the difference, in tapping, between *piano* and *pianissimo* (very soft) and *forte* and *fortissimo* (very loud).

Tempo

If the children have done the rhythm activities and clearly are interested in the Italian terms, you could follow the *piano* and *forte* exercise by singing and tapping the songs slowly (*lento*), quickly (*allegro*) and very quickly (*presto*) and introduce these musical terms.

Moving to Music and Dancing

Moving to music is an extremely valuable natural human impulse that is healthy for many reasons. After being shown how to use a CD player (that has been adjusted to keep volume low if necessary) children can be free to play and to move to music at any time just as with any other work.

A child, who has had all of this experience exploring sound and rhythm and moving free to music, will be ready to learn to dance. In some countries this is part of every child's education. In others it is wonderful to be able to introduce some simple steps to cultural dances of other countries.

In-House Concerts

Concert manners are easy to learn in the classroom. They should be short and very casual. First talk about just what a concert is, a live musical performance in front of an audience. If we have any residual fears from childhood about such a thing, we put them out of our minds because our children do not have them.

Explain that when we go to a concert we enter the concert hall quietly; we sit quietly in chairs and watch and listen to the performer without talking. When the performer is finished we applaud and leave the concert hall quietly. The performer usually bows to the audience at the end of the performance. If possible later, in class, we approach the performer and tell him that we enjoyed the music.

Create the performance space with a child or a few children by deciding where, in an out of the way part of the room, the performer will stand and the audience will sit. Next, line up chairs for an audience. With a few children, quietly sit in one of the chairs with your hands in laps and mouths closed. When the audience (one child or several) is ready the teacher can perform first when first introducing these concerts, singing one song for example. Or a child who has decided he wants to give a concert, or several people can perform at one concert. When each individual performance ends the performer bows, the audience applauds, and when everyone is finished all slowly walk out of the concert area and back to work, some helping to put the chairs back where they belong.

When I was teaching at one point the children began to arrange concerts of one or more performers; they decided what the concert would include and made programs that were passed out as we entered the concert area.

One year I had a very quiet and shy little girl who, after a concert of one child playing a little piece on the piano, signaled with one hand for me to bend down and then whispered in my ear, "Can I dance?" I was quite surprised and of course said yes. The next day she arrived with a small blanket, the tradition blanket of the Ojibwa Native Americans. Her family are members of this group and she had attended many pow-wows and I am sure danced with her friends.

Together we arranged the chairs and invited a few children who were not busy. She stood in front of them exhibiting no shyness at all, hummed the traditional Ojibwa chant and slowly, one foot placed after the next, walked in a small circle. It was clear when she was finished as the humming and the movement stopped. She did not bow to her audience as some children do after they have performed in our little concerts, but the children applauded especially quietly, matching the energy of her gentle dance, and her face glowed with happiness.

I attended a lecture at the AMI International Congress in Prague by a good friend who has been for many years an AMI Montessori teacher for older children. He told us about one of his students, a young lady who was extremely nervous about one of the few assignments, which was to give a presentation to her classmates. She was just too afraid. But finally she asked if she could sing the presentation. He hadn't known that outside of school she was active in theatre and singing. I saw the video of her presentation. She did it, and did it beautifully and with confidence.

What a lesson for all of us in the magic of music.

RECORDED MUSIC

CDs of Ethnic Music

Since there are many musical traditions on most continents you will need several, but only put one from each continent on the music shelves at a time. I had a folder for each continent (except Antarctica) with an image of the continent on the front of the folder.

During a consulting with a school in the Bahamas I helped the teacher set up this system of music from different traditions. Then I was amazed to see the reaction of some of the children. I had studied both belly dancing and salsa dancing and I could see that when a child played salsa music the child was making exactly the same body moments that I had learned when studying salsa! The same thing happened when putting on a CD of Middle Eastern music; the children made the same body movements that I had learned when studying belly dancing! That taught me a lot about how the dance and music traditions must have been intricately connected as music and dance developed throughout centuries.

CDs of Famous Composers

There used to be a perfect series of CDs that interspersed a few sentences of the life of one composer with short selections of his or her most well-known and recognized pieces of music. I have not seen it for many years but there may be something like it available. If not it is fine to have a little folder with the picture of the composer on the cover and a CD of his or her music within.

CDs of Solo Instruments

The Suzuki music CDs are very good for this. In our family we have studied Suzuki piano, violin, and viola and as this system of learning music is called "the mother tongue" method we listened to the music before attempting to play it. Each CD has very beautiful selections and only one instrument. Of course it is possible to find others. For example have a CD of Spanish guitar music with a picture of an acoustic guitar on the front of the cover.

THE MONTESSORI BELLS

All of this work provides a wonderful introduction to music for this stage of development. It also lays the foundation for the work with the Montessori bells, or for learning to play an instrument such as the piano or violin. The Montessori Bells were developed to give experience and the refinement of the sense of hearing, following the sound boxes sensorial materials.

There is an out of print book written years ago by Anna Maccheroni, a colleague of Montessori, "Developing the Music Sense: The Montessori Approach to Music for the Ear, Voice, Eye, and Hand."

The use of the bells is too extensive to be included here but it is part of any AMI Montessori primary, 3-6 course.

Through this material a child learns to match sounds, grade the sounds of the octave, the chromatic and pentatonic scales; and as he is learning to write and then read in other areas of the class he learns to write and read music. He will learn to write and read music notation in the treble and bass clefs and also flats and sharps.

In my training it was an easy step to learning the tone bars where one can transpose to a different key but this material is most often found in elementary, 6-12 training courses now.

LANGUAGE

(See the Language chapter for details and illustrations)

Stories

Learn to tell true stories to children about composers and musical instruments. Mozart is a good place to begin because there are many children's books about him. But children always prefer a short and interesting story about a famous person when he or she was a child that you can tell from memory.

Vocabulary

Give the exact names for the percussion instruments that you have in the environment, and the parts of the percussion instruments if possible. And continue to use the vocabulary that was introduced in the music activities such as the terms *piano* (soft) and *forte* (loud) in talking about a recording a child might have listened to and is telling you about.

Pre-reading Classified Pictures

I usually had two kinds of matching picture cards for musical instruments, one for traditional musical instruments from around the world and another for instruments one would find in a Western classical orchestra.

Although there are many ways to classify musical instruments generally at this age we give three: wind instruments, string instruments, and percussions instruments. You could have three sets of cards for these three classifications.

When I had placed a CD of music by Bach or Chopin next to the CD player in the music listening corner I would place the picture of Bach or Chopin, from the set of composer pictures, next to the CD player, giving the name when the child asked.

Classified Pictures Reading Stage or 3-Part Cards

These can be made of any or all of the classified pictures sets above. Also if the child has become familiar with the pictures, stories, and music of a few composers you could make a set of 3-part composer cards to practice reading the names of the composers.

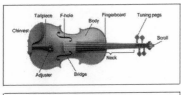

Pictures Showing "Parts of" the Musical Instruments

Parts of a musical instrument could be made in the same way as those in other areas. They can be made as three part cards, or large cards with labels such as the picture above.

Definition Reading Stages

These follow the list of Classified Pictures Reading Stage above.

Be sure that the child has heard the definitions of different kinds of instruments in conversations and perhaps had the definition booklets read to him before he is invited to read them. This is for the child that is just beginning to read sentences.

FURTHER ACTIVITIES IN THE WORLD OF MUSIC

Making Musical Instruments

As children learn about the three classifications of instruments they might be inspired to create their own. For example blowing through a straw and squeezing it in different spots is a kind of wind instrument. A string instrument can be made with rubber bands on a board with nails pounded into it. Or with a longer rubber band stretched over a small box. The shorter, tighter string will create a higher pitch. And there are several ways to make percussion instruments. Filling several identical glasses with differing amounts of water will produce different musical pitches when struck gently with a wooden chopstick.

Concerts out in the Community

Generally at this age, we bring the world into the classroom rather than taking the children out into the world, as is done a lot at the elementary level. But there might be exceptions, taking the older children out into the community for special musical events. Be sure that the concert is not too long and that it will be interesting to the children.

Museum Visits

Also, if the older children get very interested in ethnic musical instruments for example, and there is an exhibit in a local museum, you could arrange to take them. Again, go first yourself to be sure that what they want to see is really there. And plan a short visit looking for specific items instead of going through the entire museum.

SINGING

This section of the world of music deserves its own place, as it is a combination of all that has been discussed above. Dance and song have for thousands of years been an everyday part of life for people all over the world. And it is part of the daily life of a Montessori class.

Here are some of my favorite quotes on the subject:

Hope is the thing with feathers that perches in the soul —
and sings the tunes without the words — and never stops
at all.

— Emily Dickinson

He who sings scares away his woes.

— Cervantes

Then the singing enveloped me. It was furry and resonant,
coming from everyone's very heart. There was no sense of
performance or judgment, only that the music was breath
and food.

— Anne Lamott

Because of her singing they all went away feeling moved,
feeling comforted, feeling, perhaps, the slightest tremors of
faith.

— Ann Patchett

If you can walk you can dance; if you can talk you can
sing.

— African proverb

And here is one of the children's favorite poems from my
own Poetry Anthology:

Be like the bird that, pausing on her flight awhile on boughs too slight, feels them give way beneath her, and yet sings, knowing that she hath wings.

— Victor Hugo

Science is discovering today the psychological, emotional, and physical benefits of singing. Although we parents and teachers have noticed these throughout the ages it is good to have our observations explained.

For example, in our family and in my Montessori classes, the spontaneous bursting into song as a child (or adult) goes about the other activities of daily life has always been a kind of barometer of happiness that I keep an eye on. If there had been too many days of that not happening in my primary classes for example, I would take a step back and see what I was missing, and what I must do to make sure that happiness was the main result of carrying out Dr. Montessori's guidance as a teacher.

The power of music to integrate and cure . . . is quite fundamental. It is the profoundest nonchemical medication

— Oliver Sacks, British neurologist, author of
Musicophilia: Tales of Music and the Brain

Everyone is born with one instrument: a voice to sing. But musical development begins even earlier. During pregnancy the fetus is aware of the voice and even the emotional state of the mother while she is speaking or singing. In the early years a child can identify musical patterns and even improvise melodies as he combines the singing of familiar tunes. Singing affects the endocrine, immune, and nervous systems and has beneficial effects on the lungs, the ears, and the brain.

Singing also benefits social inclusion and communication, and supports a healthy self-image.

Singing, as with dance and all of the other work in the primary class, should be available to the children at any time of the day. It should not be a required all-group lesson led by the teacher. In the general knowledge chapter early in this book you can read more about this.

In the first part of this book you can see ideas for constructing a "Formal Language Book" that contains poems, nursery rhymes, songs, singing games, finger plays, and action rhymes. All of these are connected with the child's exploration of language and music, and they give him the tools to express himself musically.

The teacher adds to this repertoire of songs weekly and might also create "song cards" of the favorite song just as with favorite poems and nursery and action rhymes. With these tools a child who is not yet able to read or who hesitates to verbalize his desire to hear or sing a particular song, can select the song card because he recognizes the picture. Then he can take it to a friend or the teacher and then they can sit down together and sing.

Most importantly, when the teacher makes her plan of what she "might" do during the coming week — part of the excitement of teaching in a Montessori class is that we can have these suggestions but because we follow the children we never know what will actually happen—singing is included every single day!

Also poetry, nursery rhymes, finger plays, and action rhymes are included in each daily plan and the children often turn these into songs of their own design with original melodies.

The teacher never knows how and when these parts of her daily plan will be included. For example one day a child will select a song card, identified by the picture, to the teacher or to a friend who will then sit down and sing the words to him. Or the teacher might gather a few students who are not busy or need direction and recite a poem, show them how to act out an action rhyme, or offer a box of song cards for each to select one. Or it might be a day where one of more children burst into song while they are sitting at a table working. But in some way music will be there.

Only in rare occasions or special circumstances (transition for going home in some environments for example) singing and poetry are done in a scheduled large group. But I have written in my book *Montessori and Mindfulness* (pages 35-38) more about the negative effect of too many required and scheduled whole-group lessons when it means children are interrupted in their protected 3-hour work period every day. We want to create an environment where singing can bubble up with joy at any time.

In Music, just as in all other areas of the Montessori environment, the adult becomes an astute observer of children, combining knowledge of the theory with knowledge of exactly when and how to offer a lesson to each child. Spontaneity and choice of singing and making music, and other activities, when matched to the child's stage of development and his interest, and driven by his inner guide, is the most important element in meeting the young human's need to develop fully.

> *We cannot know the consequences of suppressing a child's spontaneity when he is just beginning to be active. We may even suffocate life itself. That humanity which is revealed in all its intellectual splendor during the sweet and tender age of childhood should be respected with a kind of religious veneration. It is like the sun which appears at dawn or a flower just beginning to bloom. Education cannot be effective unless it helps a child to open up himself to life.*
>
> — Montessori, Discovery of the Child

THE WORLD OF ART

The place best adapted to the life of man is an artistic environment, and that, therefore, if we want the school to become a laboratory for the observation of human life, we must gather together within it things of beauty.

— Montessori, Spontaneous Activity in Education

Art has many aspects in the Montessori environment. It includes not only the art created in the class by the children, but the beauty of the rooms themselves, the color of the walls, the lighting, the decoration with plants and pictures on the wall. The quality, beauty, and precision of the Montessori materials themselves set the standard, as do the way these materials are kept in perfect repair, clean, and attractively arranged on the shelves.

The main work in the art area of the classroom is to give the child the tools to express his feelings and his ever-expanding interest in and understanding of the whole world. Of course it follows that, just as all of the other work in the Montessori primary environment, this work will give opportunity for deeper and longer periods of concentration, improved visual discrimination and eye-hand control, and more concepts and a richer vocabulary for verbal communication, and skills in writing and reading.

We support the child's experience in art appreciation and creativity by providing models of art from different cultures and different periods of history, and then by giving exact techniques in the use of art materials so the child can express his own developing awareness of the world.

Art expression with these materials is connected to all other areas of the classroom as you have seen in the rest of this book: physics, botany, zoology, geography, history, and music. When we do not give adult-created outlines to fill in or a project to imitate, it is thrilling to see the inner workings of each individual child revealed in his artistic creations.

PREPARATION OF THE ENVIRONMENT

The objects surrounding the child should look solid and attractive to him, and the house of the child should be lovely and pleasant in its particulars; for beauty in the school invites activity and work . . . It is almost possible to say that there is a mathematical relationship between the beauty of his surroundings and the activity of the child; he will make discoveries rather more voluntarily in a gracious setting than in an ugly one.
— Montessori, *The Child in the Family*

An attractive, colorful, clean environment in general is a most important part of preparation of the environment in art. There should be flowers and plants in the classroom. Bits of sculpture and collage are nice. All of these things should be changed often so the children do not become immune to their beauty, and to keep them interested in such things.

There should be a section of the classroom where the materials pertaining to art are kept together. All of the art materials should be kept clean and in good repair as should the shelves where they are kept.

Have a storage cupboard for yourself—out of the classroom rather than on shelves that clutter and compromise the beauty of the environment—for extra paper, paints, and so forth.

Keep all of the children's art materials on open shelves, with a special place for everything, paints, crayons, collage material, printing equipment, paper cutting materials, etc. It is nice to have an easel and room to keep it set up on a plastic floor mat, and a little table to keep the brush and paints and plastic apron. Also have a floor cloth and bucket for cleaning up after painting. A special table for clay work is also nice to have set up. Be sure to include in your art area a few aprons, as they are necessary in several activities, and materials for cleaning, wastebasket, etc. Follow the Montessori practice of having only one of each activity.

You will have art books with stories about artists, etc., and classified cards for art, but you might want to keep these in the book or library corner, perhaps with a special section just for art books and cards.

Pictures on the Walls

Have beautiful pictures of representational (realistic) or abstract art, from all periods and cultural and ethnic traditions. Also have beautiful photographs including 2-dimensional representations of 3-dimensional art such as sculpture. Include pictures of great artists and well-known art masterpieces.

Art is always hung at the height where the children can best enjoy them, and no adult level art above this. These pictures are hung so that the center of the image is level with the eye level of a child. Change the pictures often so they will continue to attract the attention of the children.

We do not hang up the children's art because the value of creating art, and this should be emphasized to parents, is the process of creating art, not the end product.

For the same reason we do not send children's art home, but keep an example of each kind for each child in a folder to send home at the end of the term.

This is especially important because in Montessori it is the construction of himself that is at the core of our work, not the written or drawn work to be praised or given gold stars of approval, and this can be difficult to explain.

Let me describe a common situation. A child takes a drawing home. The parent is very pleased because it provides a little window into something the child did during the day. The drawing is praised and the child is happy to please the parent. The next day he remembers this and quickly creates a piece of art with no purpose other than to make his parent happy, and no real effort of deep concentration. This is not the kind of creativity that is helpful in the development of the child but it is a natural impulse and important to explain to parents that avoiding this situation is why we do not regularly send work of any kind home. We want a child to create art, or write stories, or do math work, and so on, for deeper reasons, from the creative impulse to express himself that comes from deep within. We want him to spend as long as he wants on creations, for his attention to detail and desire to do the very best work to be satisfied.

Books

Books about great artists, especially about when they were children

An art book about sculpture, Rodin for example

A child's book about visiting an art museum

The "Mommy It's a Renoir" series of books for creating folders of art cards

Origami or kirigami books with the easiest examples of traditional Japanese paper folding or paper cutting

A book of beautiful photographs of interest to a child

Books of art in individual countries, such as Chinese art, Australian aboriginal art

Art method books for working with clay or tile

CARING FOR THE ART AREA

Activities related to caring for art equipment and also books and related equipment:

Washing a table

Washing paintbrushes, water jars, mixing dish

Wiping a palette clean

Sweeping and mopping up

Sweeping after paper cutting

Washing hands

Straightening art shelves

Dusting art shelves

Washing the painting easel

Washing the plastic cloth under the easel

Washing the plastic apron used in painting

Carrying, handling, and handing scissors to another

Handling art books

A PERSONAL EXAMPLE

As in all areas we are sure that this is a useful, real example of important work that the child can manage. Then we analyze the steps and practice them before presenting the lesson to a child

Cleaning an Art Shelf

Material: a floor mat, dust cloth, spray bottle of water, drying cloth

Presentation:

Have the floor mat spread out on the floor next to the bookshelf; the books from the shelf have been neatly placed on it. The child has already learned how to spread out, or unroll, the floor mat, take things from the shelf and put them back. Have the spray bottle and drying cloth ready.

1. Show the child the thumb and first finger of both hands.

2. With these grasp two corners of the cloth and spread it out on the shelf.

3. With the right hand firmly grasp the spray bottle near the top.

4. With the left hand point out the hole from which the liquid will emerge and aim it toward the cloth, about 8 inches from it.

5. While still holding the spray bottle in the right hand, lift your index finger and place it on the spray button.

6. Push it down just for a moment, making the release of the button very exaggerated. This process may have to be done with two depending on the size of the spray bottle. Best is to find a small one.

7. Place the spray bottle on the mat.

8. Lift the cloth again with both hands and turn it over.

9. Fold it into fourths (the child has already learned this with the folding cloths).

10. Take the folded cloth in your right hand and move it to the back left hand corner of the shelf.

11. Move the cloth across to the back right hand corner of the shelf.

12. Repeat this left-to-right movement several times, moving each time a little closer to the front of the shelf.

13. The child can go on to do the next shelf if he likes.

14. When the shelf is cleaned, or the shelves are cleaned, replace the spray can to the shelf where it is kept.

15. Show the child where the used cloth goes, probably in the classroom laundry basket for someone else to wash it and hang it up, and someone else to iron and fold it and put it away.

16. With the child feel that the shelf is completely dry and then replace the books.

Control of Error: The whole shelf will look pretty, clean, and neat if the exercise is done well.

Points of Consciousness:

1. The child should have had experience with a spray bottle or be shown it in detail, especially where the water comes out.

2. He must not hold the button down too long or too much water will come out

3. The child must already know how to carry materials, put things on shelves, lay out a floor mat, and fold a cloth. If not, review or introduce these things with this lesson

Purpose:

Control of movement, eye-hand coordination, care of the environment

A way for younger children to get to handle things they are not yet ready to learn to use.

Cleaning a shelf, along with many other practical life activities is a first social act, being part of a group that works together to maintain a beautiful environment for each member.

Age: 3 years on

Note: This was one of the most popular activities in my classrooms and probably at least one shelf was cleaned every day or so, making it almost unnecessary to do a major cleaning during vacations.

SENSORIAL KEYS

There are other materials in the Montessori primary environment that prepare children for awareness of beauty, and skill in creating art. These include the rough and smooth boards, geometric cabinet, and color tablets in the area of sensorial materials.

The metal insets in the language area are also considered sensorial keys to the world of art: lightness of touch, eye-hand coordination, control of the pencil, practice with the pincer grip, and development of the hand, wrist, and arm in preparation for beautiful handwriting. Metal insets should NOT be used as templates for art projects with smiley faces and so forth. Be sure that the metal insets are used ONLY in the precise way they are presented to help the child develop the above skills.

If children begin to misuse the metal insets in this way they can be redirected to the art shelves. In my primary classes I encouraged children to make their own imperfect but individual geometric shapes so they would not be limited by such aids in creating art. I also sometimes kept a small shapes template on the art shelves so children could create art with the kinds of geometric shapes they learn about with the geometric cabinet and metal insets.

ART ACTIVITIES

To confer the gift of drawing, we must create an eye that sees, a hand that obeys, a soul that feels; and in this task, the whole life must cooperate. In this sense, life itself is the only preparation for drawing. Once we have lived, the inner spark of vision does the rest.

— Montessori, *The Advanced Montessori Method*

Art activities such as drawing, painting, paper cutting, and clay, provide the child with the experience of creating art using his senses of sight, and touch, and even what is called the stereognostic sense which means the combining of more than one sense. For example, when a child has shaped something with clay, he will have insight into what went into a piece of sculpture that he might see in the wall, or with art cards, or in books.

Drawing

Materials, one set of each, always available:

Large crayons

Small crayons

Soft black drawing pencils

Colored pencils

Plain white paper

Thin white paper for rubbings

Materials available for older children or special projects:

Non-toxic felt tip pens

Charcoal

Colored chalk

Pastels and fixative

Colored paper

Practical Life:

1. How to handle the materials

2. Where to put a finished piece of art. Usually in a folder with the child's name. Alternately you can ask the child to bring it to you and you write the child's name on the back, not on the front, and he can put it in a general storage folder

3. How to sharpen a pencil or peel the paper surrounding crayons

Presentation:

1. Drawing is connected with all of the other work in the classroom. When a child wants to express by means of drawing we show him how to use the chosen materials.

2. Illustrate soft and other pressures to get different results with the materials

3. Show how to make a rubbing over a textured leaf or other flat but textured object

4. Show how to look at an image in a book or in real life (a shell, leaf, vegetable, etc.) and draw (the child's) interpretation of it.

Points of Consciousness:

1. Do not judge or praise or ask for interpretation of what the child has drawn, as with any other art. The impulse and reasons and meanings are within the child. If it seems that the child wants you to comment you can say something like, "There is a lot of yellow in this drawing." Not, "What is this?" or, "How pretty this is."

2. Do not draw a picture for the child to paint. And do not use outlines of coloring books.

3. Occasionally you can suggest that a child draw something he is talking about such as what he saw on the way to school or what he did on a visit he is talking about.

4. Just as writing should come from the child's own experiences and words, drawing should come from the child's mind rather than being given an adult-made model to copy.

5. In suggestions of what to draw include all of the areas of the classroom, physics experiments, leaves, parts of an animal, and so on.

Easel Painting

Materials:

An easel. I have seen ones recently where a child can actually be seated and the easel is halfway between being vertical and horizontal. This enables a child to spend more time on his artwork.

A plastic floor mat under the easel

A bucket and sponge for cleaning the easel and mat, etc.

Tempera paints, primary colors of red, blue, and yellow, also back and white

Good quality brushes of different sizes

Presentation:

1. Show the child how to put on the painting apron

2. How to attach the paper to the easel

3. How to dip the brush into the paint and then wipe it on the edge of the container so the correct amount of paint remains on the brush

4. How to remove the paper from the easel and where to put it, carrying it correctly

5. How to clean the apron, the easel, and the floor mat.

6. How to clean a brush and position it so it will dry correctly

Later Presentations:

1. You might want to begin, with a very young child, showing all this with just one color. Then go on to all primary colors.

2. Next show how two primary colors will make a secondary color. Red and yellow make orange. Red and blue make purple. Blue and yellow make green. Show color mixing

carefully in a container, then the child can use both primary and his choice of a secondary color to begin.

3. White and black will make shades of one color. This is advanced work and should be presented carefully for an older child.

4. Do not draw a picture for the child to paint. And do not use outlines of coloring books.

Point of Consciousness:

Cleaning up after easel painting is very valuable work and enjoyed by the children. Don't rush through it but carefully present each step. This is a good example of a long cycle of activity for a young child. Sometimes the many steps of cleaning up after painting becomes the real work and provide even more concentration than the actual painting.

Watercolor Painting

Materials:

Good quality watercolors

A watercolor pan for mixing colors with water in separate containers that may be included in the watercolor set

Plastic table mat

Thicker white paper than for drawing

Watercolor brushes

Presentation:

1. Lay down the plastic table mat, then the paper, then watercolor set

2. Show the child how to mix one color with just a little water and then try it on the paper.

3. Then show how different amounts of water make different shades of the same color

4. Show the child that he can paint a picture freehand or he can draw first and then paint

5. Show the child where to put the paper to dry and then clean up the watercolor palette and brushes

Points of consciousness:

1. After washing a watercolor brush it should be laid on its side to dry, not stood up, to protect the ferrule.

2. Do not draw a picture for the child to paint. And do not use outlines like those found in coloring books.

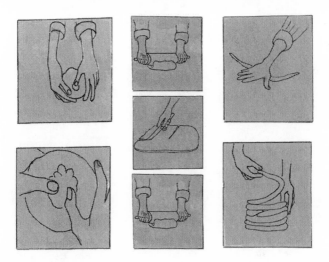

Clay Modeling

These directions are for using real clay. Using plasticine, which does not dry out, is similar. That is what I usually had in my classes,

Material:

Apron

Wooden board or greaseproof paper taped down

Water, to moisten the clay

Clay stored in a plastic bag in a container with a lid so it doesn't dry out

Wooden spoon handle or tongue depressor for smoothing

Blunt knife for cutting

Wire cutter. (This is a piece of wire tied between two sticks to draw through the clay breaking it into smaller pieces)

Wooden rolling pin

Presentations:

1. If clay has become hard, sprinkle it with water periodically, starting a few days before you are going to use it so the water is absorbed. Keep it sealed in plastic.

2. Take the clay from the bag and place it on the board.

3. Roll it around on the board pressing down until it becomes pliable.

Here are the three main ways clay has been used over thousands of years and all of them should eventually be presented to the child.

Pinch Method:

1. Roll a piece of the softened clay into a small ball.

2. With both thumbs keep pressing into the middle until a small bowl is formed.

3. Experiment with large and small pieces, thick and thin sides of the bowl.

Coil Method:

1. Roll a piece of the softened clay into a small ball.

2. Flatten the ball with your hand or with the rolling pin to make the base of a pot.

3. Form another ball, and then roll it into a long "snakelike" shape.

4. Press one end of the snake onto the base of the pot.

5. Slowly wrap the snake along the edge of the base, pressing the clay slightly into the base so it becomes attached.

6. Continue making snakes, attaching each one to the last one and forming the sides of the emerging vase or container.

7. The coils can be flattened with the wooden spoon or tongue depressor, moistened, and the vase dried. Or leave the coils showing.

Slab Method:

1. Roll a piece of the softened clay into a ball.

2. Flatten the ball with the rolling pin.

3. With the knife cut a square to be the base of the container.

4. Repeat to make four sides.

5. Fasten the base and sides together by pressing the clay together

Decorating:

Designs can be scratched into the wet clay. Let the creations dry out in the room for at least a day. They can then be painted with watercolors or other paints. Don't try to fire such rough-made objects, as they will contain air bubbles and cracks that will cause them to come apart in the kiln.

Printing

Children can make pictures, patterns, book covers, birthday cards and gifts.

Choice of methods:

1. Printing with various objects such as corks, leaves with raised veins, half of a Brussels sprout, bits of corrugated cardboard, etc.,

2. Printing with little bags of grains such as peas or rice wrapped in small bags of fine, thin, cotton

3. String blocks

4. Potato blocks

Materials for 1, 2, and 3:

1. Saucer with a small sponge in it. This is the paint pad that holds the paint. The various objects will be pressed onto it to make the print.

2. Saucers to hold the paint

3. Paint

4. Newspaper for practice

5. Good quality paper for printing, smooth at first, and then watercolor paper for textured prints

Materials for 4:

1. The above materials

2. A potato (note: it only will last for one day.)

3. A suitable small knife for carving the design

(A large knife for the teacher to cut the potato in half)

Printing with Objects:

Show the child how to pour the paint carefully into the saucer and then dip the various objects carefully into the paint, holding each above the paint to be sure it is not dripping, and then pressing it onto the paper.

Printing with Bags of Grains:

The fabric must be thin enough so the shape of the grains will show in the print.

The bags can be made ahead of time and put on a tray on the art shelf. Or older children can even cut the fabric and create the bag, tying them off with yarn or fastened with a rubber band.

Show the child how to dip the bag and make the print.

Printing with String Blocks:

A piece of linoleum or thick cardboard serves as the base. With waterproof glue, attach some thick string in a design. The sections of the string should not overlap each other as you make this design. You may use different thicknesses of string but only use one thickness per each print block.

Dip the prepared block into the paint and press on the paper.

These may be made by the teacher at first, just one on the art shelf at a time. Older children will learn to make their own.

Printing with a Potato Block:

The teacher cuts the potato in half ahead of time and places both halves on a tray with the small knife for carving. The potato will only last for one day so put it in the compost at the end of the day.

The carving can be very simple, just a small hole carved into the middle will make an interesting "doughnut shape" print. Older children will be able to make quite interesting designs.

As the other methods, carefully dip the potato block onto the saucer of paint and print.

Note: sometimes children will want so much variety in design and color that you can keep slicing the last design off of the potato half and use the same one several times.

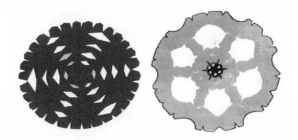

Paper Cutting

Children can make decorations such as snowflakes and stars, individual dinner mats, pieces to combine with collage work, cards

Material:

Scissors with blunt ends

Pencil

Ruler

Compass or prepared cardboard circles to draw around

Paste

Construction paper

Thin colored paper

Tissue paper

Presentation:

It is best to introduce each child separately to the various aspects of paper folding and cutting, and to supplies and practical life activities involved. A young child will need practice using a ruler, compass, and scissors, doing very simple activities before he is ready for the other activities. Have him draw a designated distance along a ruler and then practice cutting a straight line. He may cut simple pictures from magazines.

Single folds:

Take a rectangular or square piece of paper. Fold it in half, draw a half of a leaf, half of a person, or half of an oval, then have the child cut it out and open it up and discover what he has made.

Band patterns:

Take a strip of paper, fold it accordion fashion, cut a zigzag at the top, or draw the zigzag and have the child cut it, open it and see what he has made. Crowns can be made in this way and fastened together with paper clips.

Patterns from circles:

Start with a circle drawn on a piece of paper and cut out. Fold it in half, in quarters, or as many times as you can, as long as a child can cut it. Cut notches out of the three sides and open it up to see what it makes. The child may want to cut several and superimpose them on each other, or paint them, etc. This can also be done with folding and cutting rectangles.

Snowflakes:

These need the help of the adult in the beginning because the circle must be folded into 6ths to make a proper snowflake design. I taught children to begin with a rectangular piece of paper first folding and cutting it to make a square, and then into sixths. We made large and very small ones for windows at Christmas time.

Collage

Materials:

Old calendar pictures or colored construction paper

6-muffin muffin pan

Scissors with blunt end

Paste

Nice paper for the collage surface

Presentation of Cutting and Sorting paper:

Show the child how to cut the calendar art or paper into strips close to .5" wide (larger for the younger child)

Cut the strips into small squares

Sort them into the muffin pan by color, red shades in one, blue in another, and so on

Presentation of making collage:

Bring the muffin pan of little squares to the table

Show the child how to draw a square or circle, or use the ruler and compass as in paper cutting

One at a time, paste the little squares just inside the outline of the square or circle

Gradually fill in the shape with squares

Further work:

Children will naturally use collage in different ways and learn to combine collage, paper cutting, and painting into original art.

OTHER ART PROJECTS

Children can use toilet paper rolls, cardboard boxes, string, to make sculpture.

Also weaving, sewing, making quilt squares and other needlework can be kept in the art area or in the practical life area.

Notes:

1. No teacher-made models for children to copy.

2. Keep a balance between the work in the art area and all of the other culture areas.

3. After the child learns the techniques in art use all of the other areas of the classroom for the inspiration of expression in art. All areas should be connected.

4. Whatever you bring into the classroom be sure to analyze the movements that will be necessary for success. Think about what skills a child will need before tackling a new art activity. And most of all practice the activity yourself, and if possible practice giving the lesson to another adult before giving it to a child.

LANGUAGE

(See the Language chapter for details and illustrations)

Stories

Learn to tell true stories to children about artists. There are many books for children available today about individual artists. But children always prefer a short and interesting story about a famous person when he or she was a child that you can tell from memory.

Vocabulary

Give the exact names for the art materials, the names of the art hanging on the walls, and the techniques for handling art materials.

Pre-reading Classified Pictures

This material helps increase the child's vocabulary and helps with classification of objects in his world. Just as other objects in the classroom you can make cards with pictures of the easel, paintbrush, scissors, and so forth. The art area has a very special system of pre-reading pictures assembled in labeled folders. These are called the art cards.

Art Cards

Materials:

Sets of art cards with images of great art, both 2-dimensional and 3-dimensional. There should be two matching pictures each of eight to ten images. If possible have extras in your storage area so there can be changes and variety over time in the sets.

Decide on a little symbol for each set of cards so that the child can sort them back into two sets as he puts them away for the next child to use. Put this symbol on the back of each picture in the set and on the back of the envelope or folder in which that set is kept.

To begin, as always working from the whole to the details, create sets of about 10 images each, kept in labeled envelopes or folders with an identifying image on the front of each. Begin creating your collection using the following categories:

Art of the world (representing all continents)

Art of the child's continent

Art of the child's country

Art from other continents

Art from other countries

Art classified by the individual continent or country

Art of individual artists (with a picture of the artist on the front of the envelop or folder)

Art images of great art sorted by various topics of interest to a child. Examples include faces in art, children in art, landscapes, different ways of painting skies, animals in art, and so forth

Art movements such as impressionism, cubism, etc.

Aim: to increase the child's vocabulary

To help inspire exploration and facilitate classification of the world, through art

Presentation:

1. Show the child a real painting such as a nice oil painting on canvas. Then show him a print of a painting explaining the difference between an original and a print or reproduction.

2. Choose one of the sets of matching cards above

3. Go through a few of cards and name them, linking them with the painting or print you have shown, explaining that these are reproductions of original paintings

4. Teach the names of as many cards as the child wants to learn, letting him pick the cards, by means of the 3-period lesson

5. The child can get these cards out at any time and study or name them

Sorting Sets:

Eventually the child can get out two sets at a time, mix them up and sort them. Then he can get out 3 sets, 4 sets, and so on.

Control of Error:

For sorting the control of error is the little symbol you have put on the back of each image and the envelope or folder.

Age: 3.5 years on

Classified Pictures Reading Stage or 3-Part Cards

These can be made of any or all of the classified pictures sets above. For beginning readers the text under each image should be simple, the name of the painting and the name of the artist or school of art, if the country of the artist is unknown.

Definition Booklets

Be sure that the child has heard these definitions, of different kinds of elements of art, in conversations and perhaps had the definition booklets read to him before he is invited to read them. This is for the child that is just beginning to read sentences.

Here are some examples of definitions in the world of art:

A painting is a work of art using colors on a surface

A sculpture is a work of art using forms made of clay or stone

Definition Reading Stages

These follow the list of Classified Pictures Reading Stage above.

More Reading

For children who are reading and want to know more create little booklets with more information about an individual artist, and so on. And provide art books with good quality colored (not black and white) reproductions of art and captions and text accessible to a child.

VISITS TO MUSEUMS

In our tiny town in Northern California there are very few museums, but there are excellent collections of photographs of early settlers and beautiful artifacts, baskets, jewelry, and clothing, made in the past and still being made by the Native Americans. Our grandchildren always go there on visits. In the next larger city there is a museum with furniture, paintings, photographs, and musical instruments from the gold rush days. And the university has created a natural history museum with many items that children can touch. So "art" museums do not have to be just for the experience of two and three-dimensional art.

Go alone to the museum first to familiarize yourself with the museum ahead of time. When it is likely to be less crowded, where are the bathrooms, what are the special exhibits, and so on.

During the visit limit yourself to one area of exploration. For example you can choose a theme such as clothing if visiting an historical museum. Or if you are visiting an art museum with mainly paintings, choose a subject such as animals or food or children. Or focus on paintings of just one artist. Of course you will have explored this ahead of time and prepared the children for the visit. It is better for them to leave the museum wanting to return and see more rather than having been overwhelmed.

However, it IS important for a child to understand the difference between an original painting and a reproduction. And it is so delightful when children, becoming aware of the difference, figure out that their own art works are originals.

This is just like when they become familiar with the early lives of great scientists, musicians, artists, and so forth, and begin to realize that someday they too will grow up and who knows what they will create.

BALANCE

I hope this book does not inspire parents and teachers to fill their homes and classrooms with a lot more materials. Please take your time and introduce just one lesson from each area to begin. Too many materials in a classroom can be over-stimulating and can impede concentration. Montessori teachers often report that when they carefully examine the environment and remove those things that were not presented during their teacher training, limiting the material to those that have been tested all over the world for over a hundred years, children become calmer and more focused, make better choices of what to do, and the level of concentration is deeper. All of this results in more happiness and success for the children and the adults.

To end this chapter I would like to share a bit about the concept of "balance". Many years ago, while in university, I worked in a bookstore. Naturally, as I straightened shelves and helped customers, I gravitated to the areas of books that I was interested in such as historical novels, art, travel. But my job included checking every single book in every single area to see if it was the last copy. My eyes were opened to more and more areas to explore. It was as if the whole world were opening up to me in a new way and I found that I was developing interests in and having conversations with all kinds of people with these other interests.

As a Montessori teacher, drawing from this experience, I wanted to be sure that my students experienced the same thing. Over the years I have observed many classrooms. I see classrooms where a teacher loves art and every other cultural area is ignored. Or one who is interested in all of the areas but somewhere along the way was told that she couldn't sing, so she shies away from singing with her children.

I believe that children are born with gifts. Yes there are certainly pre-natal influences and DNA traces of certain abilities. But one child might be born to be a great artist, another to discover a new species of plant of animal, another to share insight into the reasons that different cultures are still eating the foods they have eaten for generations. We must not hold these children back.

In all Montessori teacher training courses, teachers are given the lessons on practical life (care of the person, the environment, grace and courtesy), sensorial materials, language, and math.

But in reality, having all of the cultural lessons in the class gives the child the possibility of caring for the environment in a new way; it gives much variety for him to explore with his senses and mathematical concepts, and reasons for learning to write and then to read that are richer than one can imagine. Let us keep this balance in order to meet the needs of the potential of each and every one of our children during this time when they want to know, and are curious about, the whole world.

> *Knowledge can be best given where there is eagerness to learn, so this is the period when the seed of everything can be sown, the child's mind being like a fertile field, ready to receive what will germinate into culture. But if neglected during this period, or frustrated in its vital needs, the mind of the child becomes artificially dulled, henceforth to resist imparted knowledge. Interest will no longer be there if the seed be sown too late, but at six years of age all items of culture are received enthusiastically, and later these seeds will expand and grow.*

— Montessori, *To Educate the Human Potential*

LANGUAGE
OF THE CULTURE AREAS

ORAL LANGUAGE

There is a saying in the Montessori world, "The adult is the most important piece of language material." This is true in the home as well as any Montessori environment. We model not only the tone of voice, and the vocabulary, but also the spirit of language. For example many of us sincerely believe that we are showing respect for a child, yet when we apply the test, "Is this the way I would speak to my best friend?" to what we have just said or about to say, we often fail the test.

Would we correct our best friend's manners in front of others at the dinner table? Would we order rather than invite our best friend to join us in an activity? Would we correct our best friend's language or remind him or her to say "Please" or "Thank you"? Would we simplify our language when speaking to our best friend, implying that he or she won't understand us otherwise? Would we stop listening to something our best friend is saying to us and turn to our buzzing or ringing cell phone? If any of this rings true, in our language as a parent or a Montessori teacher of children at any age from infant community through high school, don't worry; recognizing the error is the first step in correcting it.

PRE-READING CLASSIFIED PICTURES

In the classroom the child has been used to hearing interesting, correct, specific language; he has begun to learn the names of all of the objects and activities in the class. Now he is ready to practice his ever-expanding vocabulary.

The purpose of the pre-reading classified picture material is to increase the child's vocabulary and to aid his classification and exploration of the world, including the sensorial and practical life materials, and the world of physics, the world of botany, and so on. We do not give children random collections of pictures, for example a set of pictures combining household objects, farm animals, and tools in the same set of pictures. The sets of pictures are classified into logical groups. When we classify the cards into groups of objects that have characteristics in common we are helping the child to make sense of the world, and to classify in his mind.

The pictures must be attractive and clear, made from photographs or realistic paintings. No cartoons or stylized images that do not give the children the real information. The background should be white and the entire animal should be visible, not just part of an animal.

Before giving a child pictures, either in books or on pre-reading picture cards, we should be sure that he has seen an example of the group of objects for which we will show pictures. If the child has seen and held or petted or fed cats, dogs, a horse, or a Guinea pig, we might introduce a set of cards of a wide variety of mammals.

A Set of Classified Pictures

The material:

Let us use as an example the zoology cards for mammals. This set of pictures of mammals contains cards, perhaps 4" x 6" or 5.5" x 5.5" (the size of metal inset paper in the Montessori class) or similar, each showing just one animal. Since the animals cannot be shown in relative size because of the great variety, such as a tiny mouse and a large horse, all animals are near the same size. That way the child can study each one carefully.

The background behind the picture of the animal must be white or another light, single color. There should be nothing but the animal showing, not even the branch on which a bird might be perched. Why? Because when one points to a picture of a robin, for example, and the picture includes the branch on which he is perched, maybe some leaves and flowers, a blue sky with clouds, in the background, there is no way for the child to know exactly what you are pointing to when you are naming "robin". We adults know how to exclude the background from the robin and focus on the robin itself, but the child does not.

Of course, if it is an animal the entire animal should be clear with no parts cut off at the edge of the picture. For example with a set of bird pictures, the head and tail and as many of the parts of the body as possible should be clear.

Presentation:

The first time, the teacher selects the set of cards, based on the child's interest at the moment, and invites the child to look at them with her. Together they talk about the pictures. If the child shows great interest and it is clear that he wants to learn the names she invites him to select three and then teaches the names by means of the three-period lesson (See glossary chapter).

The culture materials that you have read about in these pages provide a wealth of language in all areas of knowledge. In each section you have seen suggestions for the accompanying vocabulary, learning the names of the real objects, and then practicing them through sets of pictures. One never knows what a child will choose to express in written form when he reaches the next stage.

PRE-READING CLASSIFIED PICTURES
IDENTICAL MATCHING

This is a set containing two of each of the pictures described above. I found that the very youngest children in my 3-6 classes loved this activity and carried it out with great attention to order and detail. They would first lay out the first set of cards vertically lining up the left edge of the card as perfectly as they could along the left edge of a floor mat. They would carefully pick out and lay the matching picture next to the first card. I put a little colored dot on the back of each picture, red for example on the back of one set, and blue on the other. Then, at the end of the exercise a child would turn over all of the cards, gently mix them up, and sort them into two sets using the colored dots as the key to doing this themselves — yet another satisfying activity. Mixing up the cards before putting them in two piles prepared them for the work of the next child.

PRE-READING CLASSIFIED PICTURES
FLASH CARDS

This is yet another use for the pre-reading classified card sets. The names of the classified pictures can be taught either in a 3-period lesson (see glossary) to an individual child, or in a spontaneous small group lesson, just holding up the cards like flash cards and letting anyone name them.

Children in my primary classes spontaneously imitated my own lesson to a child. One child would hold up, one card at a time, a set of 8-10 cards, "testing" a friend to see what names he knew. The first child would put the ones named correctly in one pile face down, and then the ones his friend still needed to learn in a second pile face down. Then the first child would teach the second child the names he had missed, mix up the cards and "test" his friend again. This was a common occurrence and the children learned hundreds of names of pictures in this way. There was no pressure; it was just fun learning new words.

Pre-reading classified cards are kept on the shelves according to the area of the classroom. Pictures of classroom materials would be found on the language shelves, but botany cards would be found in the botany area, and so on. Some sets of cards will be rotated and not kept on the shelves and some sets of cards will have internal changes. For example, a set of pictures of garden flowers might contain 10 flowers, but the teacher has more in storage and will occasionally remove some flower cards and replace these with others, keeping the child coming back to learn the new vocabulary.

Some sets of cards should stay on the shelves permanently because they represent the basics of a culture area; they represent well-rounded general knowledge for the child. For example one will always have, in the zoology area, a set for each of the five classes of vertebrates: fish, amphibian, reptile, bird, and mammal. There will always be a set of musical instruments in the music area, and the basic botany picture sets in the botany area, as examples.

Moving from the general to the specific applies also to this material. The child always has a general set of fish, but there can then be added more specific sets of fish such as tropical fish (that might live in a class aquarium) or kinds of salmon, or fresh water fish, or ocean fish, and so on. There could be more classification of animals such as farm animals, desert animals, varieties of dogs, and animals of one's country. These sets can be rotated in and out of the classroom but always have the basic five vertebrate sets available.

WRITTEN LANGUAGE
THE MOVABLE ALPHABET

Writing often comes before reading in a Montessori primary class. But this is not "taught". The Montessori teacher learns the stages of development and supports them in this area as in all areas. For example, in order to be able to write beautifully, first the development of the whole body is attended to; next the development of the hand. The child learns that what he has to say is important. He learns to recognize isolated sounds of his language through games, and he learns what those sounds look and feel like by use of the sandpaper letters. And then the child, not the adult, decides when and what to write about. The culture area gives the child a lot to draw from. He might want to list fish or dogs or food or clothing. Or he might just want to write a letter.

Here is another example from my own experience, this time as a grandmother. A few years ago our grandson visiting from Oregon returned from a visit to the local marine lab all excited about what he had just seen. I asked him, "Would you like to write about that."

With eyes wide in disbelief he clearly wanted to but didn't think it was possible at his age so together we got out one of our favorite puzzles, the lower-case alphabet puzzle. Although he was learning the letters in cursive in his primary class he had already learned the sounds of the letters of these pieces of the puzzle. "Octopus" was his first choice and with a little encouragement he figured it out "octopus." He wanted more.

"Okay," what else did you really enjoy watching in the tanks?" and with great enthusiasm he replies, "The seahorses!"

As there were not duplicate letters when he found that he needed a second "s" I said, "Don't worry, I will make one for you." Which I did with paper and pencil. Then he went on to write the seahorse woman and the seahorse man, phonetically of course.

But the most exciting moment of the day, perhaps of the whole visit, was when his mother came to see what we were doing. And when she read back the words he had written, pronouncing them just the way he had written them, his eyes opened wide with surprise and pleasure. This is the magic of humans at any age, to be able to put down one's thoughts and have them read and understood, through time and space, by another human being. This is what we want our children to experience.

In the Montessori classroom there will always be language materials called the movable alphabet, a box containing small compartments each with several of each letter. So rather than beginning to write boring, simple, three-letter words such as cat and hat (as we probably did as children), the child can begin with the important words and ideas from his own head.

WRITTEN LANGUAGE
WITH PENCIL AND PAPER

At the same time that a child might be expressing his thought through the movable alphabet he will be improving all of the skills necessary to be able to write with a pencil. These are two different things and are not combined by copying with pencil what one has written with the movable alphabet. It is up to the teacher to prepare the child, but the child decides when and what to write.

Years ago I noticed one of my students, who had not yet written anything spontaneously, wrote something and then get up to use the bathroom. I walked over to his table and looked at the paper. Here I will share what he wrote. In order to help you understand the message I will keep his phonetic spelling (quite normal at this stage for a 4-year-old) but will separate the message into words:

doent tuch mie wrk ie wil bee riet bac

(Don't touch my work. I will be right back)

Asking a child to write before he can write in a way that he can be proud of just solidifies the wrong way of writing in the brain. And it is difficult to unlearn what has been learned, stored in the brain, incorrectly.

I learned the importance of not "practicing something badly" as I learned to teach Suzuki Piano Book I. The traditional way of learning the simple song "Twinkle, Twinkle, Little Star" on the piano might be to play it, with mistakes of all kinds, over and over and over, hoping someday that there will be a miracle, the mistakes will disappear on their own and it will sound beautiful. But with authentic Suzuki music instruction the child listens to tapes of this music every day and absorbs it just as he hears spoken language daily. Then he learns how to sit at the piano, well balanced and with feet flat on the floor. He learns how to hold the arm and hand and the fingers correctly and how exactly to touch the keys. And, miracle of miracles, he plays beautifully from the very first notes until the whole piece is learned. It is the same with learning to write in the Montessori classroom. Let the child write, from the very beginning, in such a way that he can be proud of his work.

Sometimes there will be a period of time where the child wants to do nothing else but write his thoughts in this way. It is a very exciting stage for the child, to think of something, such as a list of what he saw on the way to school that morning, to write it down, show it to another person, and have his very own thoughts spoken aloud by another. This happened in the very first Montessori experiment in Rome so long ago and happens today. We call this an explosion in learning and we follow the child.

Eventually a child might want to practice beautiful letters and words, we can show him well-written examples of short poems or sayings or other snippets of language, or the language of the cultural material, to copy if he desires.

READING
CLASSIFIED 3-PART CARDS

Reading aloud is a very complex operation. Because we adults have very little trouble reading something aloud we sometimes don't realize what it feels like for someone who is just beginning to read. The new reader is doing several things at one time when being asked to do this: look at the individual letters and remember what sounds they make, see if there are any "puzzle words" that do not follow the rules of sounding out a word, expressing one word or series of words with a voice that can be heard by another person AT THE SAME TIME as going through all of the above steps to sound out the next word.

In Montessori classes we do not ask beginning readers to read aloud. Instead the early reader will be matching words to matching pictures and then checking his work to see if he has sounded out, read, the word correctly. He can then practice reading at his own pace, in his head, and then control and correct his errors without having to ask another person if he has done the work correctly.

This "Control of Error" is an important concept. This is of value because repetition is important to a child as he learns and he will often want to check his work and then repeat the activity over and over.

A Set of 3-part Cards

Material:

These can be the same pictures as in the pre-reading collection.

A set of cards with a picture and no labels, a set of matching cards that are labeled, a set of small labels.

Presentation:

First be sure that the child already knows the names of the objects shown in the set of cards. You can talk about the cards at the beginning of the lesson to be sure about this.

1. Show the two sets of cards. Place the labeled cards upside down in a pile.

2. Show him how to lay out the "unlabeled" cards on the left side of the floor mat as he has done before, but this time leaving a little space (I usually showed the first two fingers of my left hand beneath the cards to show how much space to leave) where the labels will go.

3. Turn over the labels so the words show.

4. Select one of the labels and then place it under the top unlabeled card, looking at the child shake your head, "no." Place it under the next card, do the same. When you come to the correct picture leave the label there and, looking at the child, nod your head, "yes." Do NOT read the labels aloud.

5. Do another label, or if the child understands, let him place the labels.

6. Now pick up the labeled cards and one by one place them next to the unlabeled cards – matching them by pictures.

7. With the child check by pointing to the labels to see if they match the labeled cards.

8. If the child has put some of the labels in the wrong places just show him how to rearrange the labels so everything is correct.

Control of Error: The labeled pictures

Note: Invite him to mix up the cards in the two sets and start over. When he is finished with the work, as with all other work, show him how to put the cards back in the container and then back on the correct place on a shelf. This "putting away" is a satisfying way to mark the completion of a multi-step activity. It is good for the child on many levels and it is one of the first social activities in the class—putting the material back in perfect condition to be used "by a friend."

READING STAGE TWO
"PARTS OF" CARDS

The real experience always comes before the label or language so before introducing this material to the child you will have had conversations about the parts of all of the different kinds of plants or birds for example. So he is familiar with the idea that parts of plants and animals have names.

These are simple drawn pictures, one on a card. A picture of the complete plant or animal, in this case a bulb, is colored on the first card. There are identical drawings for each part, but on each card just one parts of the plant or animal is colored in, usually in red.

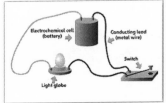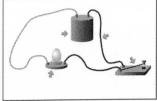

READING STAGE TWO
"PARTS OF" CHARTS

Here we can use physics as an example. While working with the electric circuit, the child has already learned the names of the parts such as wire, light bulb, battery, etc.

A Set of "Parts-of" Charts

Material:

Two charts, one with the parts labeled, one with no labels

A set of small labels

Presentation:

1. Show the child both charts, one with names and one with no names, discussing the picture and reviewing the names. The child should be comfortable with the names.

2. Place the chart with names upside down so nothing shows and explain that we will use it later.

3. Show the child the labels

4. Read one of the labels and place it where it goes on the chart.

5. Invite the child to continue

6. When all of the labels have been placed, turn over the chart with names and check the work

Control of Error: the second chart

Note: Culturally specific charts can be made. For example children in Amsterdam are very familiar with the parts of a bicycle and even the different kinds of locks and the parts of a lock. Children in Mongolia will know the vocabulary connected with the *ger* or *yurt*.

READING STAGE THREE
DEFINITION BOOKLETS

Each 2-page spread in a booklet has a picture on one page and a definition on the facing page for each concept. They are usually hand made, the pages and cover laminated, and fastened together with little rings. Alignment of text depends on the language. Arabic text is aligned right, Japanese is aligned at the top of the page, and English is aligned left. No text is aligned in the center.

Botany booklet – For example picture of a root would be on the left page and the definition of a root on the right.

"Parts of" booklets – In zoology there would be an individual booklet for each class of vertebrates. So for example the booklet for the reptile would have a picture of a tortoise, colored in, on the first page and the definition of a tortoise

opposite the picture. A picture of the tortoise with only the head colored on the left page and the definition of the head on the right.

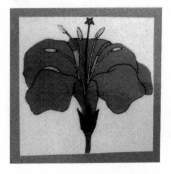

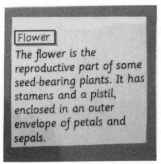

Flower

The flower is the reproductive part of some seed-bearing plants. It has stamens and a pistil, enclosed in an outer envelope of petals and sepals.

READING STAGE FOUR
PICTURES AND DEFINITIONS

Be sure that the child has heard these definitions in conversations and perhaps had the definition booklets read to him before he is invited to read them. This is for the child that is just beginning to read sentences.

When a child has heard the names and definitions used casually ahead of time by the adult then using the cards with labels with definitions will be a very enjoyable experience. Work with the botanical cards, reading stages, increases the child's vocabulary and reading ability as he learns more about the world of plants.

This set contains a picture card and a definition card that match the pages in the definition booklet.

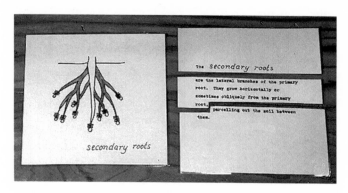

READING STAGE FOUR
PICTURES AND DEFINITIONS CUT INTO 3 SECTIONS

This material is just like the above "definition "stage except the definitions are cut up and the child has to reassemble the definition.

Material, example 1: Picture cards, definition cards cut into only two or three sections.

Material, example 2: picture cards, the same definitions but with each sentence on a separate strip of paper.

Presentation, example 1:

1. Show the child how to lay out the pictures in a vertical column.

2. Next take out the entire set of cut up pieces of definitions and spread them out on a floor mat so they are all visible.

3. Look at the first picture, go over the definition together, and then show him how to find the pieces of definitions and assemble them.

Note: The first clue is that the name "plant", "stem", "root" etc., will appear so the child will usually match these pieces to the picture first. When there are only one or two pieces left to match to a picture, the length of the sentence or phrase is also a clue

Presentation, example 2:

Present the work just as you did with example 1. This gives practice in reading and thinking about entire sentences as the definition is assembled next to the picture. I seldom see this second method in classrooms but it was in my training and I used it successfully because it gives a child practice in reading complete sentences.

Control of Error:

When the child is finished, show him how to compare each assembled definition with the one in the booklet.

Summary

Before spontaneously beginning to write with a pencil, and begin to read with great pleasure, we prepare a child in many ways so that even those first attempts at writing will be something he can be proud of. Enjoying reading is a natural outcome that follows enjoyment in writing. Here are some examples of this preparation:

Model polite, interesting, and correct language, in speaking and reading to the child.

Listen to the child so he learns that what he has to say is valuable.

Provide plenty of "formal language" stories, poems, and non-fiction, to increase vocabulary. Make reading aloud in the home, including non-fiction, a regular family activity.

Provide lots of practical life work to prepare the child's whole body and hands, and sensorial work with knobs so the child will hold a pencil correctly from the very beginning.

Play sound or "I Spy" games to casually introduce practicing in hearing the sounds that make up words.

Provide correct experience with carefully tracing sandpaper letters.

Show how to use the movable alphabet to express the child's thought, not limiting this "writing" to simple words represented by objects or pictures, "cat", "bug", etc. You can start him off with suggestions such as what he had for breakfast or saw on the way to school, but his writing attempts should not be dictated at this stage. They should be fun and exciting.

Wait till the child wants to write and to not rush it by having him copy what he has "written" with the movable alphabet. Writing with the movable alphabet and with a pencil are two completely different activities representing two distinct stages of development of the mind and the hand.

Provide correct use of metal insets, for lightness of touch and careful vertical lines, not for artwork. If the child starts to use the metal insets for art redirect him to the art materials.

Be sure the table and stool or chair allow a child to sit with good posture.

Provide good quality pencils, both colored and black pencils, colored and white chalk. Also writing with other art materials and in sand. Blackboards and paper should be of the best quality possible.

Know how to help a child who chooses to write with his left hand.

Which script? Cursive is faster to write and print leads to more errors in writing, but these days most young people cannot read cursive so prepare your children to succeed with cursive, print, or my favorite, Italics.

abcdefg
hijklmn
opqrstu
vwxyz

This script above is from the book *Montessori Read & Write, A Parents' Guide to Literacy for Children, by Lynne Lawrence*, Executive Director of The Association Montessori Internationale (AMI).

This is the font we used in my training and I used for sandpaper letters, and the first movable alphabets. It is a type of Italic cursive sometimes called Sassoon after Rosemary Sassoon, an expert in writing, especially for children. With this font children won't mix up letters such as "b" and "d", and the little "exit strokes" prepare children for hooking letters together as they write so they only need to learn one font, rather than both cursive and print. It is similar to the font used in Italy in the first casa dei bambini with Montessori when the children spontaneously began to write in a lovely way.

When a child begins to write show him how to decorate the margins of the paper, making the work even more something to be proud of.

Reading comes later. You have given the child an introduction to the world and of books. Through writing he has begun to be excited about the written word, and the fact that thoughts can be shared without being spoken aloud.

The primary class teacher introduces writing by carefully and slowly writing the name of an object in front of the child. There are just two "object boxes", one with short words where each letter can be easily sounded out, "pot", "vitamin", "clip", etc. The second with double counts such as, "quilt", "brush", or "spoon". In a home where a child does not attend a Montessori school, it is interesting to use many more objects for this stage, foods, kitchen objects, toys, etc. Be sure to model the most beautiful writing in front of the child.

Remember that learning to write and read is not a requirement in the primary class. It is something that the child will see others enjoying, even if he does not choose that work when we would like him to.

But keep in mind that before the age of seven the child is in the absorbent mind time of life, and he learns through the senses and movement, so if he can be prepared in all of these ways writing and reading will become part of him. This is not the kind of tedious work that you and I might remember from school; it is just daily, natural life. After age six reading and writing are not so easy, so let's take advantage of what we know about children of this age.

As Lynne Lawrence says in her book mentioned above:

> *Don't be tempted to rush her. Your aim is to help her develop a love or reading and writing so that throughout her life she will choose to read and choose to write.*

So we continue to check on our providing the preparation listed above and do our best and then we wait. There will come a time, on each child's on schedule, not ours, when a child will quite naturally begin to write on his own — notes, lists, stories, letters, poems — in such a way that his personality is expressed, his interests are recorded, his thoughts are shared, and he can be proud of his work. And most children who are prepared in this way will turn into insatiable readers and writers. Believe in the child.

CULTURE FOR 0-3 AND 6-12+

Most of this book focuses on the child from age 3-6 years. This chapter will consider—for each of the cultural areas—of what comes before the primary class years and what comes after.

For everything there is a season. Each stage of development has unique potential for physical, mental, and emotional development. The goal of Montessori is to continue to learn about the development of human beings from pre-natal to old age and to match the way we help a child learn to his stage of development

The purpose of Montessori communities for children from birth to age three is NOT to prepare the child for the primary class; it is to fulfill the needs of the human from birth to age three. Likewise, the purpose of the primary, or 3-6 class is NOT to prepare the child to enter the Montessori elementary, age 6-12, class, but to fulfill the needs of the child through his sixth year.

Most of all, a Montessori education is NOT merely a way to get ahead in academic accomplishment. The high level of academic work that one sees in authentic Montessori environments is a by-product of a system that focuses on observation of each individual child and adapts the environment to support the compete development of the individual—physically, mentally, and spiritually

THE CHILD FROM BIRTH TO THREE

The child in the first three years of life has an absorbent mind; he learns or takes in everything, every detail, every word, every attitude, in his world. He does this easily and completely and without mental effort. He is interested in learning about the real world. This is not the time to give fantasy because the real world is what is interesting to him now.

THE CHILD FROM SIX TO TWELVE

At this period of life the child wants to know how everything works, why things are the way they are. This is a steady growth time of life, unlike the rapid growth and many changes in the first six years, and after age twelve. The child learns through imagining far into the past and future and out into space. He works together with friends to make plans and explore the classroom and the community. He can accomplish a lot of academic work

The Montessori elementary teacher is well trained in combining art with history and geography, and all other lessons for the child. A child does not learn best by listening to someone talk, or in any other exposure to the results of someone else's research and creativity. She must explore and create on her own. At this stage children make beautiful timelines, charts, three-dimensional creations and other expressions combined with research and excitement in all areas of the curriculum. If a child becomes especially interested in the arts, its history or its graphic, or three dimensionality, the Montessori teacher is trained to help the child follow his interests.

PHYSICS

Physics has to do with matter and the properties of matter such as weight, temperature, hardness and softness, sounds, gravity, buoyancy. Physics, and all other subjects, are approached differently as we follow the interests and stages of development of children.

Physics from Birth to Age Three

From the very first days the infant is already interested in light and dark contrast and in color, and how exciting it is to be able to pull a string on a wall lamp, as I saw in an infant community in Sweden, and turn a light on and off. This is physics. Soon he will learn about hard and soft, heavy and light, by touching and holding objects in his hands. This is physics. In the first months he has been exploring the world through his eyes and ears and is curious to see what things feel like when touched and handled.

As the child progresses in his mastery of moving his body he learns about the effort it takes to lift his tummy off of the ground, and then to turn over, and then to sit up (not always in that order). And eventually he will learn to pull himself up to standing and to walk on two feet, an amazing feat of balance that took thousands of years to develop. This is physics.

When we give a child toys made of natural materials such as wood, metal, rubber, cloth, instead of plastic we not only help the environment but we provide a rich variety in temperature, weight, and textures that lead him to explore further.

He explores gravity. Think of the child who is sitting up at a table to eat with the family for the first time and drops his spoon on the floor. Then the adult picks it up and gives it to him and he drops it again. Our first thought is that he is being "naughty" but no, he is experimenting with gravity. He holds an object in his hand, releases it, and magically it falls to the floor, every single time! Think what it might feel like if we held an object in our hands, released it and it quickly moved sidewise and landed on the wall, or moved upward and landed on the ceiling.

Watching how water pours is endlessly fascinating to this child and there is great value in exploring the world of physics by playing in sand and mud and stomping in a puddle and watching the droplets of water fly into the air. Daily contact with nature — wind, sun, rocks and ocean waves, clouds, rain and snow — is physics.

Physics from Age Six to Twelve

In the primary class children have been introduced to concepts of physics in a sensorial manner. In the elementary class, thanks to this sensorial introduction, they approach physics in a new way. In "pouring air" in the primary class the child watches with wonder as bubbles of air rise through the water. In the elementary class this will be connected with the very creation of the universe and the earth. The difference between rising air and sinking matter will inspire a hypothesis. Then an experiment will be designed and the hypothesis tested and the results recorded, perhaps leading to a new hypothesis. At this age the study of matter is explored by means of charts, experiments, research into the very greatest examples such as suns and black holes, to the very tiniest construction of a molecule and how different elements combine and separate and react to stimuli.

BOTANY AND ZOOLOGY

Botany and Zoology from Birth to Age Three

A child is always aware of how we treat our natural environment, both plants and animals.

In giving the child mobiles in the early months we use objects that move in the way they would in the air or water. For example the objects hanging from the mobile represent birds or butterflies or fish, rather than elephants or horses. Thus the infant is learning, as the mobile gently moves in the air current of the room, how these animals would move through air or water. This is the first zoology lesson. An aquarium is often found in infant communities and children learn to care for the fish by feeding the correct amount of food, putting the needs of the animal first, sometimes even a 2-year old can be found cleaning out the aquarium.

This is the time to introduce fruits and vegetables, to be seen, handled, squeezed, cut open and explored inside and out. Children can participate in gardening and in a Montessori infant community they learn to dust and wash the leaves of plants and how much water to give them. Flower arranging is a common activity in the Montessori community at this age and the absorbent mind takes in the language of flowers, fruit, vegetables, and all other kinds of plants.

Botany and Zoology from Age Six to Twelve

Just as with the physics experiments, the botany experiments give children the sensorial experience of the needs of plants — heat, light, water; and he experiences phototropism, sprouting seeds, and watching the growth of plants. These early sensorial experiences create a respect for, and love of, the natural world, which inspire questions in the elementary class where the older child is more interested in, "why and how things work". From age 6-12 he learns about how the planet changed over millions of years and how this affected the evolution of plants and animals. He learns in detail about photosynthesis, and chemistry of the growth of plants, the internal functions of animals now and how they evolved, the needs of both plants and animals, and finally about ecology and the balance of all life forms. The knowledge is not gained by teacher lectures or assignments but by carefully planned and tested methods — through the use of impressionistic charts and timelines and experiments — of sparking curiosity and the desire to know more about the natural world. Children set their own goals, individually and sometimes small group projects, and learn how to realize them.

THE WORLD OF HUMANS

Here we consider the subjects of history, geography, art, and Music.

The World of Humans from Birth to Age Three

The child's experience in arts appreciation begins at birth by the arrangement of the home environment. The colors and textures, light, clothing, dishes, furniture, quality of toys, artwork, and plants, become part of the child's artistic sensibility.

In the first three years the child will internalize the language and attitude, the colors and art and music and tastes, of the culture into which he is born, and any cultures to which he is exposed in the early years. The absorption of culture occurs easily in the home and planned for in the Montessori infant community where the child exists in an environment rich in a wide variety of ways to experience the beauty of the human-made world.

The World of Humans from Age Six to Twelve

The history, geography, art, and music materials and lessons covered in the AMI Montessori 6-12, or elementary, training is so vast and deep that teachers have to be very careful not to turn it into a curriculum to be assigned, lectured about, and covered completely by every child.

LANGUAGE

Language from Birth to Age Three

Language in this context includes spoken language but also the language of music, dance, and expression in art.

Even though he might not speak all of the languages to which he is exposed, his brain will be processing and storing the sounds and he will begin to understand the meaning.

In today's world where children are exposed to screen time where they see other people talking to each other but he is not involved, and where he observes adults talking to a phone or just to the air with little electric devices perched on their ears, it is very important to give the child experiences observing people talking politely to each other, and listening to each other with patience.

We must rekindle the child's feeling that what he has to say is important, more important than whoever might be contacting us through a phone. We focus on making eye contact when he reaches out to us, even positioning ourselves in such a way that our face is on the same level as his, listening without rushing or providing the word he might be searching for, until he is finished.

Just as in the primary class, we focus on the child's daily life, vocabulary and pictures of clothing, food, parts of the home, and transportation. These are the things he wants to learn about and talk about. And these will be the basis for how history and geography is approached in the primary class.

So that the child has something to observe and express, verbally and through dance and song and drawing, we can provide a rich cultural environment, full of experiences in language, music, dance, and art.

Language from Age Six to Twelve

The study of language at this age is combined with the study of humans over thousands of years. What was needed first, nouns or verbs? Why did people first draw pictures on caves? How and why did language spread over mountains and across the seas?

Giving a presentation is much different in a Montessori class than a traditional class — one child standing in front of the group and reading. Children learn how to read with expression, with much practicing, sometimes being videotaped to study themselves, and then delivery. A presentation can be more than just words, combined with pictures, movements, art, music, and even dance.

Then a child, on his own or with a few friends in the elementary class, decides to follow a particular interest to research and then present to the group. There are no limits. I can think of many examples.

In one of my 6-12 classes a child used the history study charts to research one of the Northern California Native American groups. It engaged him so completely that he researched several groups and shared what he had learned to the class with music and pictures and even some of the native language. In another 6-12 class I observed a group of students preparing a presentation of the process of photosynthesis, taking the parts of the leaf, the sun, water, and carbohydrates, and dancing the process.

It is important to keep in mind that, even though there are bare bones requirements for children at this age depending on the country or state, the Montessori lessons are not a curriculum, they are offered just like a child is invited to a lesson in the primary class. One of my favorite parts of teaching in 6-12 classes was that even though I helped the students create "suggested work" weekly or bi-weekly plans, I never knew each month what was going to be created, but I knew each creation would come from the child's curiosity and it would be presented in an interesting and unique way.

THE NEXT CHAPTER
MUSIC THROUGHOUT LIFE, ONE CULTURE EXAMPLE

So far in this book you have seen different ways that all of the elements of culture are introduced to children from birth to age twelve. In the next chapter, The Music Environment from the Beginning to the End" you will read about how just one element of culture, music, can be enjoyed throughout life. How music is absorbed, is studied, and how it fulfills human needs from early in life through adult life will be described. This is a reprint of an article published by the Association International in Amsterdam.

When you finish reading that chapter, think about how every other element of culture—physics, botany, zoology, history, geography, and art—can be enjoyed throughout life.

THE MUSIC ENVIRONMENT FROM THE BEGINNING TO THE END

By Susan Mayclin Stephenson:

AMI JOURNAL 2014-2015, Theme Issue: The Montessori
Foundations for the Creative Personality

*S*usan *Mayclin Stephenson became interested in children very early in life. At age nineteen she travelled around the world on the maiden voyage of The University of the Seven Seas studying, among other subjects, a sociology course on childhood and education, during which she visited homes, schools, orphanages, and hospitals in Europe, the Middle East, North Africa, and Asia. This interest in children and other cultures is a combination that has kept on motivating Stephenson all her life, as a mother and educator.*

Stephenson has a bachelor's degree in philosophy, a M.Ed., and AMI 0–3, 3–6, and 6–12 diplomas. She has taught ages two years through high school and serves as an AMI course examiner. She is the author of multiple books including The Joyful Child, The

Universal Child, and Child of the World, No Checkmate, Montessori and Mindfulness, and creator of the Wonderful Two's DVD.

The natural urge to sing, dance, make and listen to music wells up from the depths of each person, from birth to death. It can be stamped out at an early age or it can be fostered to enrich all of life. This article describes how important music is to us at every time in our life, from birth to death. But, what is music? What words can successfully describe it? We might as easily try to capture all the most poignant sights, sounds, and smells of childhood holiday celebrations into a single black and white collection of letters on a piece of paper. We may not know how to describe music, but we do know that we don't want our children to miss out on it.

I have heard fascinating presentations by Dr. Adele Diamond, neuroscientist, both at the Annual General Meeting hosted by AMI in Amsterdam (2010) and at the AMI Educateurs sans Frontières (EsF) Assembly in Thailand in 2015. Her contribution to the Montessori movement of nurturing children is significant because she studies how executive functions—including the ability to think outside the box, mentally relate ideas and facts, control impulses, and the ability to concentrate—are affected by biological and environmental factors.

Recently, she has turned her attention to the possible roles of music and dance in improving not only executive functions, but also academic outcomes, and mental health. In many a talk she passionately argues that there is a very essential reason why dance, play, storytelling, art, and music have been part of human life for tens of thousands of years and are found ubiquitously in every culture; perhaps we have discarded the wisdoms of past generations too lightly.

> *We need to look back. There was wisdom in previous generations that we're ignoring. We think we're going to be "modern", and that we can do better than our parents and grandparents. There are things that have been part of the human condition for thousands of years — that have been part of the human condition for good reason; otherwise they would have been weeded out.*
>
> — Adele Diamond

Music is made of vibrations felt by the ears and by the whole body. The lower notes, the longest and slowest vibrations, are felt by the human body as touch. Beethoven in his last and very productive years as a composer was completely deaf. His solution to continue hearing was to have the legs removed from several grand pianos; he composed by sitting on the floor, feeling the vibrations from the piano strings and the piano wood enter his body through the floor. Today technology has been developed that can do the same thing for deaf musicians. The effects of different pitches, intervals, and timbres evoke different responses in us. Part of this phenomenon is cultural, but it is also psychological and physical. In my training with Silvana Montanaro she reported on experiments with plants that show us that the music of Mozart and the Indian Ragas support growth and health, while loud rock music can cause death. Wisdom from the past says that there exists a music of the spheres, as electrons spinning around the nucleus of the cell and as the planets spinning around the sun. Laurens Van der Post discovered some of this wisdom as he got to know the Bushmen or *San* of the Kalahari:

> *As long as the Bushman heard this sound of the sun and stars and could include it in the reckoning of his spirit, all was well in his world. The howl . . . reached me and seemed to change into a minor scale the major key of the music of the stars which resounded over the vast full-leafed garden beyond.*
>
> —Laurens van der Post, *Witness to a Last Will of Man*

MUSIC AND THE STAGES OF LIFE

Prenatal

From the first cell, the human infant begins life in touch with music, with the rhythms of the mother's body. As he grows up, his experience becomes more focused, more refined, sensitive, and educated. Montessori teachers are devoted to keeping the development of humans as close to the natural plans as possible in all areas from birth on, and to do this we must do all we can to keep the child in touch with music. He is the human link with the universe, the past, the future, all of nature, and with each other.

It is a combination of many different sound vibrations that the child hears in the womb. The rhythm, the pitch, all of the subtleties of sound are taken in by the developing human, in ways we do not yet understand. The child is constantly exposed to, and responding to, the internal sounds of the mother's body and the external sounds of the larger environment. Many cultures of the past understood this enough to have the best musicians play for the unborn child and for the mother to sing a special song to each yet unborn child. Scientists today can trace the specific muscles that are stimulated by specific sounds. Language tapes played before birth may stimulate the "music" of a second language and improve the child's ability to learn both after birth. Many mothers know that children keep time to external music by kicks and other movements and that a piece of music sung or played often enough before birth will be recognized by the child after birth and can have a calming effect on him.

Just as the child moved in response to sound in the womb, he does this after birth. Notice a joyful baby kicking his feet wildly because someone is talking to him. It may be that this movement begins to lessen in response to spoken language, but it definitely continues in response to the elements of music.

Birth to Age Three Years

Just as in the womb, the newborn child responds to sounds and other experiences, such as a loud crash or a familiar face with his whole body—clenched fist, thrown-back head, great smile accompanied by wildly, joyfully kicking legs, or sometimes the motionless stillness of focused attention and study. Perhaps the lack of music in our culture at this stage accounts for the fact that this movement expression tapers off as our children grow, whereas it continues in children from cultures where music and dance are a daily part of life. Percussion instruments provide more variety in the natural inclination to move and clap rhythms.

Maria Montessori spoke of this period of life as the time of the 'unconscious absorbent mind'. During these years the child literally 'becomes' what he finds in his environment. The human brain has a dedicated set of nerve cells that respond only to the sound of music, and scientists believe that if these have not been stimulated by eight months, they will start to die off at that time. We already know that certain sounds can be detrimental to health whilst others are supportive. Therefore, a great responsibility rests upon us to examine carefully the sounds in the child's environment.

In the first few months of life the child begins to make music with his voice. I have often had the joyful experience to begin a singing dialogue with a child at this age. When the child makes a cooing sound, we can repeat the pitch, the time, the length of the sound. Very rapidly, the child will catch on and begin to make a variety of more and more sounds intentionally. If we carefully imitate these attempts, longer and longer joyful duets of music will result. This is a very important experience in the development of the child's self-image, his attitude toward communication, a preparation for singing and talking.

In the early days and months a child is attracted to faces and carefully watches the faces of the person who's talking and singing. When we change or bathe the child, it can be disturbing if we distract the child with toys, or rush the task. It is better to relax, smile, and explain what we are doing while looking at the child's face. Slowing down and involving the child gives a feeling of respect, of belonging, of communicating, and it provides a wealth of vocabulary about the child's world. If we sometimes sing this communication, we give a wider range of pitch and the vocabulary of music. This is interesting to the child and he will focus and listen. These moments of dressing, changing, and bathing provide important quality time for communication between adult and child.

When I was taking the AMI Assistants to Infancy course in Denver, Colorado, during out breaks I would play a piano that was in one of the course rooms that I played when there was a break. I remember Dr. Montanaro, my trainer along with Judi Orion, coming into the room with a slightly distressed look on her face. At first I thought maybe the music was disturbing to others, but then she said, "We must find a way to let the children in the Infant Community in this building watch and listen to you."

This brought home a very important point she had made during one of the neuropsychology lectures, that from an early age children should be shown music being created by the hand and the movement of the human body.

Since then, having been brought up in a family where everyone played an instrument, I have been very surprised to discover that many children have never seen this. When music always comes out of a car radio, or a CD player, how can children be inspired to pick up an instrument and learn to make music? Wherever I go now in international work I look for ways to share this experience, by matching percussion sounds or playing a piano, when I can find one. Even the youngest child, as in the picture above, delights in being shown how to touch and pull on a guitar string gently so that the sound is the same as when the adult does it. Children at this age are interested in using their hands, and in movement of all kinds.

As adults we have the ability to shut out unpleasant sounds, but the child does not—he hears everything. One day I was in the bedroom reading to our very young grandchild. Suddenly he looked at me and said, 'Bird!' I put the book down and listened and could hear some crows far up in a tree outside our window. I would never have heard them if my grandson had not shared his experience with me. In the home and the Montessori community we should pay special attention, not only to what can be seen, touched, tasted, and smelled, but also what the children hear. If the child is in an environment where the sounds from a TV, a passing car, a wind-up toy, music from the radio, the running of a dishwasher, etc. can be heard, this is the "music" the child will become accustomed to and will want to recreate in his life. If the child grows up with this cacophony, he will continuously try to recreate it in his life, no matter how detrimental it may be to his body, mind, and spirit. If he is in an environment of peace and quiet, soft beautiful voices and lovely music, he will recreate this in later life and be nurtured physically and emotionally.

In the Montessori Infant Community the children have a strong sense of order, not only of place or environment but also of schedule. Montessori mornings can often end, after a snack or lunch, with singing. The teacher is also very likely to sit down at any time of the day to give a language lesson to one child or to sing a song with one or two children. Because children are not required to come to these lessons and because they love the language and music many, if not all, will participate. They are free to go back to other work at any time. Concentration on independent work is always considered more valuable than group experiences. The period of these first three years is the most intense in all of life for storing up sensorial experiences. We do not talk baby talk to the children, because we know that this is the time when they are absorbing the music, grammar, and vocabulary of the language they are exposed to daily. For the same reason, we do not limit their musical experience to baby music.

As long as we carefully observe the children and their response to the music we offer, there is no limit to the music we can provide.

Age Three to Six Years

During these years the child learns to sort, classify, and arrange the sensorial experiences that began in the first three years; he learns to organize the brain and make the information available for creative expression. If supported by the environment, children at this age can easily and effortlessly learn to write and read music and play instruments. It is thought that rhythm instruments were the first used by early humans, and this is a good place to begin with children. In their hunger for spoken language

this is the easiest time to learn the names of pieces of music and composers, not for this information on its own, but so that they can ask for and talk about the music of their choice. As we give children the elements of culture it is quite natural that we give them the music of all cultures.

During my AMI 2.5–6 training at MMI (the Maria Montessori Institute, now MMTO, Maria Montessori Training Organization) in London, I did part of my student teaching in a school in St. John's Wood. One day I saw a very young child walk up to the teacher, look up at her and, as the teacher bent over to be closer, whisper something in the teacher's ear. Of course I couldn't hear the words, but from what followed I think she said, 'Can you give me a dancing lesson.' I often tell this story today when I am consulting with a school where help is needed to implement the three-hour work period that is required in an AMI school. I hear, 'But when will we sing? When will we dance? When will we read books or tell stories or share poetry or nursery rhymes or finger plays that we are supposed to do every day.' My reply is to 'follow the child and do them at any time during the day with one child, or a few children, but never on a schedule.'

Let us return to the dancing lesson. Together the teacher and the young child cleared a small space in the classroom by moving a table and a few chairs. Then they removed their inside slippers and placed them under one of the chairs. Together they went to the tape player (this was before CDs were invented) and selected a tape, put it in the player and turned it on. The music played quietly and the two of them danced, in the style of the greatest of modern interpretive dancers, to the rhythm and energy of the music. When it was clear that the child was finished they put their inside shoes back on, put the tape back in the box of tapes, and the chairs and table back where they were. Everyone in the classroom around them had continued with their work undisturbed so it was clear that this was a common event, a one-to-one lesson.

There are many old and traditional songs that have appealed to children throughout the ages. But the first six years of life, the absorbent mind years, is the time to expose children to the music of their own culture, of other cultures, and the classical music of the West, which in turn was influenced by the music of many non-Western cultures; just think of Ottoman martial music, which was in vogue in Vienna during the eighteenth century. Also Satie, Debussy, Ravel, and other French composers were influenced by Javanese gamelan music, and Gustav Holst's opera "Saavitri" was inspired by the Indian classical Rig Veda.

Akbar Kahn, a Hindustani classical musician from India, preferred Indian music to all others. His second choice, however, was the music of Bach and Beethoven. The last five hundred years of the development of music in Europe have been the most varied and profound of any on earth. Everywhere in the world, one hears music from this tradition, which acts truly as an international language.

During my A to I (birth-to-three) training our family went to Rome. We stayed at a convent where preschool children attended classes during the day. Our son asked permission to practice on the convent piano. As he began to play western classical music the children from the preschool came from their classroom and gathered around the piano, humming along because they were familiar with the classical music he was playing. Then, as he began to play the music from modern American composers, their attention wavered and they started to wander back to their classroom; they couldn't relate to this music. They were very pleased when, a few moments later, he returned to classical music. We had similar experiences years later with visitors from Sweden. The children spoke very little English and communication and play was stilted until the parents realized that all three children were Suzuki students. Just the humming of a few of the Suzuki pieces caused the curtain of strangeness and isolation to fall away and a feeling of belonging to the same community took its place.

One year I was consulting with a school in the Bahamas and helping to create a music appreciation set of music CDs representing each of the continents of Asia, Africa, North and South America, Australia, and Europe. The owner of the school already had a fine international music CD collection so it was easy to select one for each continent. We labeled the front of the CD case with an image that matched the colors and shapes from the continent puzzle map. Children were free to select and play any of the CDs at any time during the morning three- hour work period, the volume control having been set on low permanently with a metal staple so the music was not too loud. None of the children had been exposed to this music but it was remarkable to see that when they played, for example, the Salsa music from Colombia, or the belly dancing music from Egypt they made exactly the same kind of whole body movements that salsa and belly dancers from those countries would make. I had studied both of these kinds of dance and so noticed it particularly, but I imagined that the same thing would hold true for the music of the other continents, the piano music of Chopin, the didgeridoo of the Australian aborigines. It made me ponder just what was the relationship between cultural music and the synchronized body movements, and where did it all begin?

Other ways to include music as individual activities

in the Montessori 2.5–6 class

Listening to Music: Silvana Montanaro who directed many AMI Montessori Assistants to Infancy courses, in her child neuropsychiatry lectures, explained that earphones can have very negative effects, both psychologically and physiologically. Listening to music on a low volume CD player should be a chosen individual activity during the three-hour morning work period. Even in the Montessori infant communities we sometimes find a little corner, perhaps with a tiny easy chair and a large plant providing privacy (and leaves to dust and wash) for a child to choose and listen to music.

Playing Musical Rhythm: To become aware of rhythm, form a small group of children, each with a percussion instrument. Teach them to play the rhythm of their names, imitating the number of syllables and the rising and falling pitches. Think about how these will sound, repeating each name five times: A.lex.an'der, Sam, Su'san, Ur'su.la, and so on.

Learning the Names of Musical Instruments: Even in the Montessori infant communities one might find musical instrument models and matching cards in the little corner where one can listen to music CDs The same thing can be used in the 3–6 class. At this age the pictures and models do not have to match in size and color, and it is also possible to match CDs of solo instruments to the pictures of the instruments, just as we match the pictures of composers to CDs of their music.

The picture above was taken in the AMI 0-3 course environment in Hangzhou, China, that was created by Maria Teresa Vidales and her daughter Teanny Hurtado.

Bring in Composer Tapes with the Story and Music of One Composer: There are excellent story tapes such as "Romeo and Juliet" and "Beethoven Lives Upstairs" for individual listening. Play music from different cultures linking them to objects, flags, and pictures from continent folders or continent boxes.

Song Cards: So that a child can ask for a particular song (of finger play, or poem, or nursery rhyme) at any time during the three-hour work period, I prepared a set of cards with one song and an identifying picture. The non-reading child can go to the box of cards, look at the picture, select the one he was looking for, and bring it to the teacher or in some cases an older child to sing or read it.

Visiting Musicians: Oftentimes a parent or a family friend will be delighted to bring in an instrument and play just a few moments for the children. Be sure and explain the 3-hour work period and that children will come to their little lesson only if they choose, so the guest's feelings won't be hurt if he or she ends up playing for only a few children in the class. Everyone will hear and benefit.

Concerts: In my school we had "concert practice". Even for the simplest song played on the bells, or me playing the piano, or a visitor, someone would make up a program, line up a few chairs, and practice good concert manners, listening instead of talking, keeping hands in lap, and clapping when the performing musician was finished and had bowed to the audience.

> *If we try to think back to the dim and distant past what is it that helps us reconstruct those times, and to picture the lives of those who lived in them? It is their art. It is thanks to the hand, the companion of the mind, that civilization has arisen.*
>
> — Montessori

FORMAL MUSIC INSTRUCTION

What about formal music education for children? For many it is not enough to learn to sing a few songs or to read and play someone else's music. Nor is it satisfying to the spirit to learn to recognize the music of musical periods and composers merely to label them and quickly move to the next. We must prepare an environment that protects and nourishes the music the child carries within him from conception.

There is a great satisfaction in learning to sing the words of a song, to write and read music, but perhaps the greatest elements of music are physical and emotional. The joy of feeling and expressing music with the whole body and the voice, of creating original music alone or as a group, and moving through space to these sounds has always been an essential element of human life. There are several child-friendly ways to introduce children to formal reading and writing.

The Montessori bells — as in the picture above taken in a 3-6 class in Moscow, Russia — are standard sensorial materials in the Montessori primary class, and children easily learn to match and then to grade them. With enough practice a child can hear a bell tone played and know the name without knowing where in the scale it is. This is a natural skill called perfect pitch that many of us thought was inborn, or was not. No, it can be learnt at this age. Sometimes children go on to learn to read music.

In our family we have enjoyed learning music with the Suzuki method. How the names Suzuki and Montessori are used can be very similar: The label can be attached to all kinds of schools and classes, which sometimes have nothing to do with either Suzuki or Montessori. It is therefore important to learn to recognize a real Suzuki teacher. There are other similarities. For example, Suzuki is called "talent education" because rather than thinking that a person is born with musical talent or not, the belief is that any child can be a good musician with the correct instruction. It is also known as the "mother tongue" method because—just as with listening—children are not expected to be able to replicate a beautiful sound on an instrument if they have not had many, many hours of listening to the very best musicians performing the simplest Suzuki repertoire beautifully. Likewise we would not expect a child to explode into perfect spoken language without having heard his mother tongue from before he was born.

Another commonality which, as a Montessori teacher I could really appreciate, was the analysis of the steps of learning, awareness of what skills must precede and what skills will follow a particular step on learning a piece of music.

One summer, as I was passing through Denver, a good friend brought her four-year-old daughter to the airport during my layover to show me what she was learning in her newly begun Suzuki violin lessons. Anne placed her violin case on a seat, carefully and deliberately opened the clasp and lifted the lid, picked up the satin violin cover and laid it over the cover of the violin case. Then she picked up the bow, tightened it and put it back in the case. She picked up the violin and carefully put it on her left shoulder holding it in place with her chin and her left hand and picked up the bow again with her right. Standing tall and proud she produced the first six notes of the first piece in the Suzuki violin book one. Next she tucked the violin under her right arm and slowly smiled and made a little bow in my direction. Just as carefully she put everything away and closed the case. I thanked her for her "concert". And she was pleased. Doesn't this remind us of the care with which any of our young children would carry out the grace and courtesy and the early movement development work in our classes?

In 1995, as I was visiting the Suzuki Talent Education Institute in Matsumoto, Japan, I was fortunate in being able to attend an opera lecture by the director of the institute. Professor Takahashi, a flutist, explained to me the purpose of his training for adults who are going out into the world to become Suzuki teachers for children. He believes that music must be first listened to, then expressed through movement of the whole body, then sung, and finally played on the instrument. During the lecture, the teacher trainees listened to a famous opera aria. Then Mr. Takahashi demonstrated the feel of the music by body movements and the singing voice. He sang neither in Japanese nor Italian, but a kind of joyful intense humming, rather like a jazz musician. The difference between the flute and violin playing of his students before and after this body-voiced expression was remarkable. Instead of individual notes his students could actually feel and express the intention of the composer and the emotion of the musician.

This is what we must pass on to our children. This is the ability with which they are born — the ability to express emotion naturally in music with the body and the voice.

Age Six to Twelve Years

The second plane is the time of stable growth and interest in the morals and reasons of everything; the time when children are interested in forming groups and working in groups is the best time to be in a music group. In the picture above a group of children of this age are learning to play the famous horse-head fiddles, in Mongolia.

It was during this time that our son formed his first rock band of two guitars, a drum set, and keyboard. The boys were so sure that they would be as famous as the Beatles someday that they labeled and filed each and every one of their rehearsals. They learned a lot of music, but they also learned a great deal about being patient with each other, not forgetting all of the other abilities necessary to work successfully together. In their search for an audience they performed at a homeless shelter and homes for the elderly where they learnt much about society as well. They were also able to give to others by making tapes of their music, which became important and much appreciated gifts for their families.

Age 6–12 is a time of steady growth, not like the years birth-to-six and 12–15, and so it is a steady time for learning to read, write, and play music. The ego is strong and the hard work necessary to make progress in any endeavor is pleasurable. Being in a musical group or an orchestra satisfies the need at this age to be part of a group and to adapt one's own needs to the collective purpose of the group.

As teachers of this age we can offer a multitude of inspiring and soothing music for these searching young people. For a child who does not play an instrument I have kept a guitar, recorder, and piano always ready with materials to help him begin to play. Even a few chords on the guitar can sometimes unlock the emotion and creativity of the adolescent.

Moving to music becomes more refined because the dances of the modern culture as well as ethnic dance from other cultures are interesting to children of this age. On the intellectual level music can be connected to history and to the migrations of cultures in the past. Many years ago our family attended a performance of the Throat Singers of Tuva, a group of four men from a small community in the middle of the Siberian subcontinent. During the performance a single man performed an ancient Tuvan dance that mirrored almost exactly the costumes, drum, movements and music of the Plains Indians of North America. The singers are convinced that the people from Tuva who crossed the Bering Straits so long ago were the forerunners of all the aboriginal Americans. What an inspiration for the elementary child to study migrations and communication between cultures.

In 1977 I taught a 6-12 class for the first time. This was in St. Croix, US Virgin Islands. The head of school knew ahead of time that I required a piano for the classroom, so the mother of one of the young ladies told me on the first day, "Pia is planning to be a vet, so you don't have to give her piano lessons."

I replied that no one would be required to learn music, but I would offer beginning instruction on recorder, guitar, or piano to any student who was interested. When I was not busy during the class time I practiced a Chopin piano piece that I was supposed to play at a wedding in Washington DC at the end of the year and Pia fell in love with it. It is eleven pages long and not easy and I could never play it without music, but working diligently, before and after school and during the lunch hour (after her fellow students complained about hearing the same piece over and over) Pia learned the whole thing beautifully, by memory, by the end of the year. She had never played a note of music before that. Almost forty years later, in 2015, Pia brought her husband and two grown boys to visit us and since neither of us had polished that piece in many years, I played a recording, Chopin's Opus 64 #2, for her family. I am sure it inspired them to continue with their own musical studies.

Age Twelve to Fifteen Years

As in the period from birth to age six, this time of life is filled with rapid growth and the need for nurturing. It is a time of both clinging to the past and rejecting it, and it is marked by a need for real, meaningful and creative work, and for peace and solitude.

Last year I visited Mongolia and was able to learn about how children are raised in the city and also out in the plains, living in *ger* (the Mongolian word for yurt) that are moved several times a year to follow the herds. One of the responsibilities of a child at this age is to learn to guard a herd of sheep and protect it from wolves. From a young age a child will go with the adult, but the mark of "manhood" is when he can manage to do this alone for long periods of time. It is these hours and days of solitude that can give rise to the greatest of the music, the poetry, and the songs, of the Mongolian culture. In the West it is rare for a young person to have this kind of solitude, this time to process and create. However in a Montessori Erdkinder, for ages from 12 to 15, spent on a farm or close to nature, it can be possible.

My personal positive memories of the tumultuous years of adolescence include walking along the river in a hot Indiana summer under the shade of oak trees singing "I'll Never Walk Alone" at dramatic full volume; and sitting in a darkened bedroom listing to Elvis Presley singing "Love me Tender, Love me True". My adolescent spirit was reaching out in ways I did not understand, but found solace in music.

Along with the modern music that teenagers crave, I have seen the music of many Western classical composers resonate with people at this age. It can be calming, but it can also mirror the tumultuous emotions experienced at this age of hormonal changes and the realization that one is part of the world and will be responsible for conditions soon. The hopeful and joyful feeling of the music of Bach and Mozart can be healing; and musicians such as Paul Hindemith, who expressed outrage at war- torn Europe, can express the pain and agony that is also felt at this age. As well as listening, there are both simple and complex ways for the youth to learn to express through one's own music, not only by the lyrics, but also by the speed, pitch, and timbre. This can give many the craved outlet for self-expression and original creativity and even an enhanced self-image that comes from being able to perform for the pleasure of others.

Many years ago I was a counselor at a juvenile detention center in California. The population was basically split between the children of poor black families from the slums and wealthy white families from the hills. Nowhere was this division more evident than in the music. The black music was full of rhythm, hope, and spirit; it made one laugh and dance and was in stark contrast to the moaning, sad drug culture music of the white child who had every material advantage but no hope. The two kinds of music they chose to listen to expressed their experience of the world, and their feelings, and as they were exposed to both kinds of music they were brought together as a group and began to learn to understand each other.

Just like music, literature and art have the power to affect us: A poet from Sweden once shared an experience with her daughter, who had been sick and was not improving. Asked what she was reading, she showed her mother a pessimistic modern novel. Her mother suggested some beautiful nature poetry and the healing began. Which literature or music is "healing" to the mind or the body of course depends on the individual, and it is worth experimenting to find the right kind.

Age Twelve to Eighteen Years and Adults

Montessori spoke of the four planes of development as the basis for her theory of psychology. If the needs of the child have been met in the first twelve years (the first two planes, birth to six and 6-12) the young person at age twelve or thirteen is reaching the first stage of becoming an adult. It can be a traumatic, hormonal few years, but when these young people are treated with the same respect given to adults, and given responsibility and meaning in their work, they will thrive. In the above picture we see young people this age and adults all playing music together on the famous horsehead stringed instruments, and on other instruments, in the capital of Ulaanbaatar, Mongolia. They do not think of themselves as children.

The music these young people play, as they are becoming adults, will be meaningful to them — as one of the positive experiences of this potentially tumultuous time, throughout life.

Music heard at different times of our lives can have different meanings because as children we stored some experiences as a syntheses of sensorial input: the sounds, tastes, emotional state, touch, all of these elements "wired together" in the brain. You may have experienced the result of this phenomenon—a musical experience in the present that unlocks the drawer of memory from the past that comes flooding back, rich in its sensorial completion. I remember a few years ago telephoning a friend and getting her answering machine. The piece of music that I heard at first shocked me. Then I felt warmth of joy flooding through my body and tears came to my eyes. The piece was a short section of a Mozart sonata that my mother used to play on the piano and I had not heard it since that time.

In our son's life we witnessed something similar. When he was ten, I happened to be playing some Scott Joplin music on the piano that I had never played in his presence before. At the beginning of one piece, his attention became riveted to the music. He begged me to teach it to him.

Although he was not ready for this music, we found a simplified version, rewrote it to include subtleties which he insisted must remain, and he worked until he learned it. What was the reason? Finally, discussing it with his father, we realized that during the summers when he was between one and four years old, the ice-cream truck announced its arrival on our street with this piece.

As adults, we all have the experience of returning to not only a piece of music, but also the lyrical words of a poem that evoke an emotion which we feel stuck inside us, which needs release. There is a poem by James Whitcomb Riley called "Little Mandy's Christmas Tree", which I cannot read without crying. I grew up in Indiana, the home state of Mr. Riley, and experienced many of the elements of this poem in my personal life. In the Montessori elementary class for children from the ages of six to twelve, one of the main lessons is about the power of language, through which humans can reach out over miles and centuries and touch the soul of another. The children asked me over and over to read this poem in order to observe my response, and to have to help me with the ending. Music, because it is more universal than the language of one group of people, has even more power to touch us.

In my own experience nothing can lift my spirits like moving to the music of the sixties or hearing beautiful music played with sincerity of emotion. The most important memories of my life are linked to music — hearing my mother play Grieg's "March of the Dwarfs", as she made up a story about Norwegian trolls having a picnic in the woods, or lying in bed at night listening to my grandmother play the harp until my sister and I fell asleep. For healing the spirit, my first recourse at any time of joy or grief is to express these emotions at the piano. This ability, and none other, is the satisfying result of years of piano lessons. When my first daughter left for two years in the Peace Corps in Africa, my grief was terrible. It bubbled up inside me until finding escape through the piano. Music has power and it is there for us.

THE ELDERLY

My mother was a musician and as she entered her eighties it was becoming difficult for her to play the harp or piano. I knew Montessori has helped the elderly in many ways for years, but I wanted to find out how to help her with music. In 2014, I saw the movie *Alive Inside*, which won an award at the Sundance Film Festival. It follows the work of a social worker who founded the non-profit organization "Music & Memory". Oliver Sacks, the renowned neurologist and author of *Musicophilia: Tales of Music and the Brain*, is one of the people interviewed in the movie. The following year it was very exciting to hear of a new group being formed by Association Montessori Internationale (AMI) to research the needs of the elderly. MAGAD, the Montessori Advisory Group for Aging and Dementia, was first presented at the annual general meeting in Amsterdam of 2015.

Later that year one of the presenters, Anne Kelly, also spoke at the EsF (Educateurs sans Frontières) assembly in

Thailand where she guided me in helping my mother. Knowing well the miraculous effects of personalized music on loved ones, Anne explained that it is the music of early childhood, the music our parents play when we are young, that is the most successful in helping the elderly. Our family then researched the music of the 1920s, purchased fifty pieces from Amazon, downloaded them to an iPod and wrote out directions for her to listen to this music on a very comfortable set of earphones. Earphones are used in this case so an elder can listen at any time without disturbing others. Recently, when I was with my mother as she listened to music, even though she has trouble remembering many things, she was thrilled to be able to remember the words and titles of songs. And a friend of hers (in the above picture) asked to borrow the earphones, and then also started smiling, singing, and tapping her feet. Anne says that this is not just for happiness, but it actually makes positive changes in the brains of the elderly.

When my father, a physicist who loved music, was eighty- four he was in the top of a tree cutting branches to allow more sun to reach the solar panels he had installed on his greenhouse. He fell out of the tree and three days later he died. In those last hours he was unresponsive but we could follow his heart rate, etc. on the hospital monitors. We brought in his favorite CDs of Bessie Smith and various jazz musicians. It was clear to everyone that he was responding to this music.

I have heard that in Hawaii the tradition is to gather at the bedside of a dying person to pray and sing. Maybe, as part of a living will, it is a good idea for all of us to make a list of our most uplifting music to escort us to the next step in a very humane way. Silvana Montanaro told us during the birth-to-three training that a crisis, even though it is usually painful in some ways, always opens one to the possibility of more freedom and should be celebrated. This is true for birth, for weaning, for learning to walk, and maybe even for death.

As we follow our Montessori way of discovering and supporting the best in human instincts and wisdom, perhaps we can keep this in mind as our elders leave us.

CONCLUSION

Humans are not just a body and a brain. There is always a part of us searching for balance and wholeness. I believe that music has a lot to offer. To quote Dr. Silvana Montanaro:

In western education we tend to separate body and brain because many of the things the right hemisphere (intuitive) is able to do are not highly valued. So, from a very young age, children do not learn to express themselves and leave that hemisphere underused, because they haven't been encouraged to give much importance to body movement in dancing, singing, and drawing, all of the arts. In eastern civilizations, however, greater importance tends to be given to the intuitive part of the brain; the logical hemisphere is considered irrelevant in solving the real problems of our existence.

A new form of education will not appear until we give serious consideration to the fact that we have a "double mind". Children at any age must be offered a balanced experience of verbal and intuitive thinking to help develop the great potential of the human mind. The results will not only include better functioning of the brain, but also greater happiness in personal and social life. The better the two hemispheres work together, the richer everything we do will be.

GLOSSARY

ANALYSIS OF MOVEMENT

Each activity the child is shown has a specific sequence of movements. Each lesson given to a child has been analyzed carefully in order to be sure that the movements are necessary and clear. This is called the analysis of movement. Part of Montessori teacher training is learning to know when a child is ready for a particular lesson. There are skills that need to be mastered before a child is given a particular lesson; there will be skills mastered in that lesson that will prepare the child for the next level of work.

ABSORBENT MIND

The absorbent mind is a mind able to take in knowledge quickly and effortlessly. This absorbent mind kind of learning is present throughout the first six years of life. Language is a good example. Imagine what kind of effort and time it would take you or me to learn a second language. But in the first years of life a child can easily, with no effort, absorb several languages with perfect pronunciation and grammar if he hears these languages being well spoken in his everyday environment. Knowledge of the absorbent mind plays a large part in the creation of the Montessori primary environment; it is the reason we give the child as much exposure to the real world as he wants to take in.

CLASSIFICATION

This means grouping or sorting according to common characteristics. Sorting by size or color, or grouping language cards into sets of only mammals, only birds, only artists, and so on. This kind of classification aids the construction of the intellect. There are many opportunities for this in in the Montessori class.

CONCENTRATION

Deep concentration on an activity chosen by the child, involving an intelligent purpose with the body and the mind working together, that is appropriate to the child's stage of development, and which is not interrupted, is the single most valuable thing we can give a child. It is an expression of true understanding and love of a child. It enables a child to get in contact with the wisdom of his deeper self, and results in happiness and kindness toward others and a level of learning that is beyond what we used to expect of young children.

> When a child begins to show interest in one of these (lessons) the teacher must not interrupt, because this interest corresponds with natural laws and opens up a whole cycle of new activities. But the first step is so fragile, so delicate, that a touch can make it vanish again, like a soap bubble, and with it goes all the beauty of that moment.
>
> — Montessori, *The Absorbent Mind*

CONTROL OF ERROR

In traditional education when a child attempts to master something it is the teacher who tells him if he has done it correctly. In Montessori classes every attempt is made to help the child be able to assess his own attempts, and to correct them if necessary. This is satisfying in a number of ways, including the fact that a child can choose what to work on and carry out the work until he sees that it is correct. This protects the child's independence and improved self-esteem and self-motivation.

> *Unless I can correct myself, I shall have to seek the help of someone else, who may not know any better than I do. How much better if I can recognize my own mistakes, and then correct them! If anything it is likely to make the character indecisive, it is the inability to control matters without having to seek advice. This begets a discouraging sense of inferiority and a lack of confidence in one's self.*
> — Montessori, *The Absorbent Mind*

COSMIC EDUCATION

In this context we use the word *cosmic* as the opposite of *chaos*. In the first six years we give the keys to open the doors to all of the elements of the world. In these years such learning is absorbed easily. At the elementary or 6-12 years, when the child has a different kind of mind, he will, in drawing on the experiences in the first six years, start to see how everything is connected. Rather than encountering a mass of unrelated information to master randomly through the years of schooling, he begins to realize that we are all connected to and in some ways responsible for each other and for everything on the planet. He learns that he too can create a way to meet his needs at the same time as he contributes to the rest.

GRACE AND COURTESY

Rather than constantly reminding a child to walk instead of run or telling him to be careful when carrying something, he is given practice and various challenges for learning to walk and to move gracefully and carefully. Rather than constantly reminding a child to say please and thank you, or to help another person, or other examples of good manners, these lessons are given first of all by the modeling of the adult, and then by games. For example, to learn not to walk on a friend's floor mat where he is working, I would spread several floor mats out, almost touching, and challenge myself and a child to walk through this maze of floor mats without touching a single one. We played little games to learn how to watch a friend who is concentrating so it was not necessary to remind a child not to interrupt someone who is hard at work. These games are created so that we can "teach by teaching rather than by correcting."

HUMAN TENDENCIES

In her years of careful observation Montessori discovered that there are predispositions that are universal and that have existed throughout history. We observe them today in human beings of all ages, their expression changing at different ages and stages of development. One of these human tendencies is exploration. The infant explores through his eyes, ears, touch, and sense of smell from the moment of birth. The child in the primary class explores through movement in the environment and with materials that help to refine these senses. The elementary child explores through his imagination and research. The adult explores through reading and asking questions, and of course Googling on the Internet.

Fulfilling these tendencies is how a person learns to meet his physical, mental, and spiritual needs. A list of tendencies usually includes exploration, orientation, movement or work, order, communication, concentration, exactness, and precision.

INDIRECT PREPARATION

This involves analysis of movement. For example if we want to show a child how to polish shoes we will have made sure that he has already mastered the abilities to take his shoe off, carry objects carefully to a table, unroll the vinyl table mat, open the jar of polish, and everything else that will help him put together all of these skills and succeed at the new one. This way the teacher can be sure that the new challenge is not too easy, but it is not too difficult. It will require attention and concentration and effort, but the child will be able to succeed.

ISOLATION OF DIFFICULTY

Isolation of difficulty works hand in hand with indirect preparation. There will be only one new part of a lesson, one difficulty being isolated. In the shoe polishing example, maybe the only new thing the child will be shown is actual application of the polish and then the brushing or shining of the shoe.

MIXED AGES

Mixed ages in a Montessori class is essential for many reasons. Children do not compare themselves with the level of accomplishments of another person. And the level of work of children is not compared one with the other by the adults.

In traditional school there will be a test given to all of the children in the class, no matter what their age or skill level, at a time decided by the teacher. The results are compared and rated and each child will get a grade based on how much of the information he has mastered at any one moment, not taking into consideration his age, interest, speed of learning, and other factors. In the Montessori primary class, lessons are given to one child at a time and are based on each child's specific interest and preparation for that lesson. Then the child repeats the activity until he is satisfied with his ability.

Another important element of mixed age groupings is that it helps the teacher avoid giving group lessons and focus on 1:1 lessons, at all ages. This fosters independence, children teaching each other instead of depending on the adult for lessons. Younger children teach older and older children teach the younger. There is nothing so valuable as teaching someone else for making one's learning solid.

In my experience I have learned that the wider the age span the more effective the class, the more independent the children, and the higher the level of learning. I often had children in my primary classes for more than four years and they never, even at almost seven years, ran out of challenges to master. In teaching elementary I found that when the age span was the full six years there was much more inspiration for the younger children because they could see the full six year curriculum in front of them. And the oldest children could realize how far they had come, how deep their learning had become, as they observed and helped the younger children in their work.

PLANES OF DEVELOPMENT

In the past children were seen as small adults with the same needs and the same styles of learning. Now we know that different periods of life have unique characteristics and needs. Through years of observation it has been shown that the first six years is one stage, or the first plane of development. The second plane is age six through twelve. The third plane is age twelve through eighteen. And the fourth plane is age eighteen through twenty-four.

POINT OF CONSCIOUSNESS

You have seen this phrase used in many of the presentations in this book. Sometimes the point of consciousness is called a pedagogical note or a point of interest. I think these three vary somewhat so I will stay with what I learned in my training and how I prepared lessons over the years.

For example a point of consciousness in teaching a child to pour water from a pitcher into another container might be that the pitcher is the correct size, and that the handle is such that it will fit a child's hands. But over the years I learned to pause while showing a child how to pour, and sometimes even make eye contact and smile just as that very last drop was slowly dripping from the pitcher. I call this slight pause to make the point to the child, a "point of consciousness", because it is during this fraction of a second that both the child and I are paying special attention, we are being conscious. This kind of attention to detail in giving lessons leads to refined control of movement, extreme care of work, and deep concentration.

PRACTICAL LIFE

In the very first children's house or casa dei bambini in Rome, Italy, Dr. Montessori discovered quite by accident that when children were given real activities to perform, things that they had seen adults and older children carry out at home, they preferred to do this in school rather than to play with the beautiful toys that had been donated by her wealthy friends. Today practical life work is still seen as extremely important in the Montessori primary class, and at all other ages. This real work, and the physical, mental, and emotional benefits, lay the foundation for all other work.

Sometimes a parent might think that his child's time is being wasted with this work, that he is in a Montessori school to get an academic head start. Thanks to research today in how the brain works, especially research of executive function—the abilities to plan, focus attention, remember, to manage oneself in order to achieve a goal—we understand more and more profoundly the value of this part of Montessori.

This is why in each of the cultural areas in this book we begin with the practical life lessons connected with this area. These purposeful activities—mopping, carrying work, washing hands, sweeping, dusting, and so much more—help the child become a valuable member of the community, learn self-control, and become a complete human being.

> *...to teach a child to eat, to wash himself, to dress himself, constitutes a task much longer, more difficult and even more tedious than feeding, dressing and clothing him? The first is the work of an educator; the second is the easy, inferior work of a servant.*
>
> — Montessori, *The Discovery of the Child*

PRESENTATION

By presentation we mean a special kind of lesson. It is not the traditional lesson where the teacher talks and the child learns, but it is a presentation of materials and a demonstration of how to use the material, followed by the child's own repetition or work.

PRIMARY CLASS

The term primary class in this context refers to the group of children from about 2.5 years old to age 6+. In some countries primary class means 6-12.

REPETITION

The need for repetition of an activity has been seen in children forever. A child might do the same knobbed puzzle twenty times, another child three times. When observing the child repeating an activity it is clear that something has happened to alert the child that he is finished working with this puzzle. Now we know that this something is called "learning."

The firing of neurons in the brain during these three or twenty repetitions occurs in the cortex. When the child has learned how to do the puzzle perfectly (at least for that sitting) the activity in the cortex is reduced and now the firing of neurons occurs in the lower part of the brain where learned skills are stored. This opens up "real estate" in the cortex for the child to take on a new challenge.

So when the child asks you to repeat a story you have told him WITH NO CHANGES that is what he is doing. If he asks you to repeat it 10 times he has a good reason.

After giving a child a lesson or a presentation the teacher always asks the child if he would like to repeat it. This is very important because it sets the stage for real learning. If it was a very long lesson where the child needed a lesson on how to end it or prepare it to be put away, you can say, "When you are ready to finish this work if you come and find me and I will show you the last part."

SENSE OF ORDER

The need for order is one of the clearly visible human tendencies at this age. Children are involved with activities with many logical steps that require intelligence and concentration. When the materials are kept clean, complete, and in order, the child can work. "A place for everything and everything in its place", one of my grandmother's sayings repeated to us over the years, now makes absolute sense to me. A great artist or scientist could not respond to an inspiration if he could not find the tube of paint he needed, or if the canvas was torn, or if he could not find the test tubes he needs. The order we see in a Montessori environment is not due to some personality quirk of an adult, but the fulfillment of an important need of children.

SENSITIVE PERIODS

These are related to the planes of development as each plane has different times when certain needs can be met and certain interests are focused. An example is the sensitive period for language mentioned on these pages, the time when a child can take in several languages perfectly. This is a sensitive period in the first six years of life. A sensitive period provides the optimum time in life to obtain a skill, and then it fades away never to return.

SENSORIAL MATERIALS

Montessori used carefully designed materials to help children understand what they experience through different senses. For example the famous pink tower, made up of ten blocks of graduated size, isolates only one variation. They are all pink and smooth and the same shape, just the size is different. Through learning to put these cubes in order by size the child internalizes, or abstracts, the idea of size. At this point he begins to receive lessons on the language of size, "large" and "small" or "larger" and "smaller" and so on, because at this time the concepts are very clear.

Scientifically designed sensorial material isolates qualities such as color, size, shape, roughness and smoothness, smell, sounds, etc. and this isolation focuses the attention on this one aspect. The child, through repeated manipulation of these objects, comes to form clear ideas or abstractions. What could not be explained by words, the child learns by experience working with the sensorial materials.

SENSORIAL MATERIALS - EXTENSIONS

This is one of the most misunderstood concepts I find in my work as a school consultant. Each set of sensorial materials provides one "key" to enlighten the child about that part of his world. When the door has been opened and the child has walked through, there is no further need for this key. The child now understands the concept and will use it in exploring the world.

When a child is bored and not challenged with work he might begin to misuse the sensorial materials, for example using the pink tower as building blocks. This should be interrupted kindly and the child re-directed. Otherwise the beautiful lessons with the pink tower will not be modeled for the other children.

The main sensorial extensions for the pink tower are these two games:

1. The child takes two floor mats and places them on the floor at some distance from each other, preferably out of sight. He places the cubes on one mat and gently mixes them up. Then he chooses the largest and carries it to the other mat, and then he continues, building the tower in this way, at a distance.

2. This game is introduced when the child is learning the language small, large, smaller, larger, smallest, largest. Again two mats with the cubes mixed on one. The teacher chooses one and carries it, accompanied by the child, to the other mat. She asks the child to bring her the cube that is, "slightly

smaller" or "slightly larger." Until all of the cubes have been brought.

SENSORIAL MATERIALS - SENSORIAL KEY

A sensorial key is something that unlocks a door to a piece of the world that can be directly experienced through the senses of sight, touch, smell, sound, or taste, rather than through the imagination. They build the foundation for later abstract thinking about the world. There is only one key necessary, so that means just one piece of materials for teaching large and small, one piece of material for teaching thick and thin.

STAGES OF LEARNING

Learning a new skill can be analyzed into three stages. The first one is the introduction; the second is the work, practice, exploration; the third is the proof of learning.

Let's take the learning of a recipe as an example:

Stage 1: read the recipe in a book or on the Internet.

Stage 2: gather all of the equipment and following the instructions.

Stage 3: prepare the recipe without referring to the directions. Or share the recipe that you have memorized with a friend.

Which stage is the longest? Well, in order to be able to prepare the dish without referring to the written recipe or to share it, from memory, with a friend without, you will have had to make it many times, right?

It is the same in the class and one of the reasons why mixed ages are so important and student-to-student teaching is so beneficial.

In traditional education systems the first and second and third stages take about the same amount of time. The college student attends the lecture or reads the assigned chapter (stage 1). Then he stays up late and memorizes the material as close in time to the exam as possible (stage 2). Then he takes the test (stage 3). And very soon he forgets most of what he memorizes. However if it is a lesson that takes a lot of practice during the second stage of learning, perhaps in a laboratory or out in the field, there is a much better chance that the student will remember what he learned.

THREE PERIOD LESSON

The three-period lesson found regularly in the Montessori primary class is based on the three stages of learning described above.

Stage I might be showing the child three or four pictures of fish and giving the name, clearly and repeated. This is the classified pre-reading material referred to in the Language chapter.

Stage 2 provides practice with these cards such as, "Can you hand me the ____", or "Would you please place the _____ picture on this corner of the table." (Pointing to what you mean), or "Please could you hold the _____ in your lap." This stage should be as long and as interesting as is necessary for the particular child.

Stage 3 is the test. You pick up or point to one of the pictures and say, "Do you remember what the name of this fish is?"

If the child makes an error in stage 2 the teacher subtly returns to stage 1. If he makes an error in stage 3 she subtly returns to stage 2.

During the Montessori training course in Morocco in 2018 I was giving a presentation of the three period lesson to the teachers-to-be. One of the students asked if she could give me a 3-period lesson using her own language, Arabic. It was very difficult for me and nothing else could have helped me understand the importance of the long second period of this lesson.

THREE-HOUR WORK PERIOD

This refers to the amount of unstructured, unassigned time during which children choose their own work and concentrate each morning, and sometimes also in the afternoon. During this time there are no regularly scheduled required group snacks or group lessons or other regularly scheduled activities. There is nothing that would interrupt the potential of the child being able to concentrate as long as he desires on the work he has chosen.

There are exceptions. In starting a new class for example there may be twenty-five children aged 3-6 with no Montessori experience. In this case there will be back-to-back large and then small group lessons as children are shown how a Montessori class works, learning to bring materials to a table mat or floor mat, to use it correctly, and to put it away. But as soon as a child or some children begin concentrating they are no longer called to these groups and eventually the lessons will all be 1:1, one child at a time and everyone will be doing their own work as it has been shown that children at this age want and need to mostly work on their own, with their friends nearby doing the same thing.

This is explained very well in Montessori's book *The Advanced Montessori Method, Volume I,* chapters "My Contribution to Experimental Science". She also explains the tendency of children to get tired in the middle of this work period for a while, called "false fatigue". False fatigue is temporary, a transition, and disappears as the children begin to concentrate more deeply and for longer periods of time.

ABOUT THE AUTHOR

I began to discover the value of Montessori philosophy after my oldest child, at age three, began to attend Gateway Montessori School in San Francisco, California in 1969. After earning my first (Association Montessori Internationale) diploma in London, England in 1971 and teaching for several years, I lectured for the Montessori teachers in Head Start programs in Oakland, California. It was then that I discovered that there were elements in my own training, found in this book, that were not always part of other Montessori teacher training programs.

Over the years, after earning AMI 0-3 and 6-12 diplomas and working with children of all ages and with parents of the very young, I realized that Montessori's vision of parents and teachers having knowledge of the whole world, and providing experiences of the world to young children — according to the age and stage of development — is more important than ever. Through this work we will contribute to the formation of a generation of people who will be able, through their own real experiences and love of the world, to protect our delicate ecosystem and build a culture of peace among people of the world.

Over the years I have shared the information in this book in many ways and many places, with my own students, in workshops and lectures from New Zealand to Ireland and even in a village in the Ural Mountains between Europe and Asia, and writing in many national and international publications.

Keep in mind how long it took you to read the book and compare it with what you would learn during the hours, weeks, and months of attending an AMI Montessori teachers training course!

The cultural subjects in this book are just one small part of a full and complete training course. One learns in detail the philosophy and practice, the practical life, sensorial, language, math, and geometry work. One practices giving lessons with other adults in preparation for giving these lessons to children. And one studies all of this under the supportive guidance of teacher trainers who have met the highest standards of excellence in their own teaching and the multi-year requirements of becoming a teacher trainer.

I offer sincere gratitude to my teacher trainers at the 0-3, 3-6, and 6-12 courses. I was a student in the 58th teacher training course at The Maria Montessori Institute (MMI) in London in 1970. Just think of all the experience that was gained by training teachers from around the world for so many years. In 2019 their 100th course will be celebrated.

My children and the children I have taught over the years, many of whom I am still in touch with even from the 1960's, have been my greatest teachers. Thank you to my husband and good friend who help with all of my books, and to all of the people who have read my work and listen to me speak because your responses and questions always serve to help me understand, at a deeper and deeper level, the value of this work.

Whether you are a parent or a teacher or just someone who enjoys sharing your world with children, I hope you enjoy using the ideas in these pages. Your love of these subjects as your world opens up will be contagious.

I first began sharing the children's cultural lessons in this book with the Headstart teachers in Oakland, California in 1985. Soon after that I presented them at a Montessori conference in Auckland, New Zealand. The physics experiments were published in the NAMTA (North American Montessori Teachers Association), and in 2019 I delivered them at the AMI 3-6 course in Casablanca, Morocco.

Many people over the years have helped make this book a reality. Since there are too many people to mention individually and I don't want to forget anyone I will instead mention the countries where these people are from so you can see what an international effort this has been: Australia, Bhutan, Brazil, China, Congo, Holland, India, Martinique, Mongolia, Morocco, New Zealand, Nigeria, Romania, the UK and the USA.

And finally, the book would never have been completed without the encouragement and patient proofreading of my dear friend, AMI 3-6 and 6-12 teacher, Helen Wills Brown, and my husband, Montessori father and grandfather, Jim Stephenson.

Never doubt that a small group of thoughtful committed citizens can change the world: indeed, it's the only thing that ever has.

— Margaret Mead, Anthropologist

Made in the USA
Middletown, DE
21 March 2021